THE SECRETS OF SYNTHESIS

ANALOG & DIGITAL

by STEVE DE FURIA

PRODUCTIONS™

Published by
Third Earth Productions Inc.
Pompton Lakes, NJ

© Copyright 1985, 1986 Ferro Productions

Book Design © Copyright 1986, 1988 by
Third Earth Productions Inc.

Produced by John Cerullo
Cover Design by John Flannery
Cover Photo by George Mauro
Illustrations by Steve De Furia

ISBN#: 0-88188-516-9

How To Use This Course

Welcome to **"Secrets of Analog and Digital Synthesis."** You have taken the first step into what will prove to be a comprehensive learning experience which, hopefully, will open a new world of musical possibilities for you.

You are about to discover that there is a great deal of information contained in this course (probably more than you ever expected). We have made every effort to present this material in the easiest to understand manner. Here are a few hints to help you get the most from this course in the shortest possible time.

Without belaboring the point of how to study, here is an easy way to use the video tape and manual together in order to master the subject matter. It can be broken down into three easy steps:

SCAN STUDY REVIEW

Scan: Don't feel you must absorb everything in one viewing. This course is equivalent to *months* of private instruction. First, get an overview of the material.

Look over the table of contents. Make notes of topics that are of particular interest to you, as well as topics that you feel you might be weak in.

Set the **tape counter** of your VCR to **zero** at the beginning of Lesson One. Sit back and watch the tape. Don't be concerned with understanding or retaining all of the information presented. There's plenty of time to review. *Write down the counter numbers* at the start of each lesson, and at any of the topics that interest you.

Take advantage of the fact that this is a video course. You can stop viewing at any time and come back later! Use the tape counter as a video bookmark.

You can scan through the entire tape in this manner, or proceed one lesson at a time.

Study: When you are through scanning, study a manageable portion of the course in more detail. Use both the **manual** and the **tape** together. You'll find that each reinforces the other. Pay additional attention to the topics that you highlighted while scanning. You will know you've reached the end of a manageable portion when you begin to lose your concentration, or your attention drifts to something else.

Review: Finally, review the material you have studied. This will reinforce what you have just learned, and allow you to absorb material the second time around.

If you have a synthesizer you will want to duplicate the demonstrations on the tape and *explore their implications.* Stop the tape and experiment! It will always be there when you're ready to move on.

Be sure to watch the tape in a quiet environment. You will need to be able to hear the difference between subtle sound nuances.

If you have some burning question which you can't seem to answer from the information presented in the course, send your question along with a self-addressed stamped envelope, your signature, and registration number. We will send the answer to you and direct you to the spot in the course that will be of more help.

Remember: Take your time. SCAN, STUDY, REVIEW

The amount of information presented in each lesson is generally too much to retain in one sitting.

The video tape and manual for **"Secrets of Analog and Digital Synthesis"** can be used as a reference source as well as a complete course in electronic music techniques and theory.

Author's Note

MAKE ANY SOUND YOU WANT...

A provocative statement. Is it a realistic possibility, or advertising hype? Actually, it is a challenge. In Volume One of ''Secrets of Analog and Digital Synthesis,'' we have assembled all of the tools you will need to meet that challenge.

It is no secret that synthesizers have become a major facet in all aspects of contemporary music production and performance. Every year, more and more synthesizers appear on the market. Every year, more and more of them are purchased. The universal acceptance of the *programmable* synthesizer indicates that musicians desire to create and manipulate *new* sounds.

However, there is a stumbling block between musicians and sound creation. At first, this stumbling block appears to be the difficulty of keeping up with ever-changing technology used in each successive generation of synthesizers. That's not really the case. The problem is even more basic than that. Musicians, people who spend their lives *immersed* in sounds, know very little about how their instruments make sounds. The traditional instrumentalist can take sound creation pretty much for granted.

Everyone knows what a trumpet, or guitar, or piano sounds like. A dedicated performer can make a life's work out of perfecting his or her ''sound,'' but they never need to know *why* their particular instrument sounds the way it does. Furthermore, for each instrument, there is a vast body of highly specialized knowledge and performance tradition. Players can draw upon these to perfect their technique.

This is not so with synthesizers. By definition, a synthesizer is an instrument that has no particular sound of its own. It is a sonic ''clean slate.'' Also, because of both the general purpose nature of the instrument and its relatively young age, there are few specialized skills and techniques available for the developing synthesist to learn from.

There is, however, a vast body of general knowledge about music and sound that the synthesist can apply, very specifically, to sound design and performance. Before he can effectively create and musically control sound, the synthesist must learn about its physical nature. Otherwise, he will be trapped into twiddling knobs in a trial and error manner, and constantly confounded by the slight technical differences between different synthesizers.

This doesn't mean it is not possible to develop an effective, intuitive approach to sound design. Indeed, many of the best musicians learn by ear. However, all musicians recognize the importance of learning rudiments at some point in their development. Even the most intuitive of musicians can benefit from studying such rudiments as scales, harmony, and ear-training. In this tape and manual we present the rudiments of synthesis — sound creation and performance. You will find that they can be applied to virtually any type of synthesizer: past, present, or future. Like all other rudiments of music, they must be rigorously studied and applied.

The material in this course will give you a solid foundation upon which to build or extend your skills as a synthesist. It is our sincere hope you will find it helpful in meeting the challenge...

Make any sound you want!

Steve DeFuria
Spring '85

Author's Notes
for Second Printing

As **"Secrets . . . "** goes to press for its second printing, I have the opportunity to make any additional introductory comments about the course that I feel will be helpful to you. The course stands on its own. The contents and presentation have not been changed. I would like to point out some general things to keep in mind as you go through the material:

★ The information is presented in a very concentrated form. Don't expect to absorb everything at once. You'll find that as your synthesis skills develop, the course will continue to be an invaluable resource, to both reinforce concepts and point you in new directions.

★ The material is organized as a *method* for sound design using any kind of synthesis technology. You will learn how to become independent from any particular hardware at the same time you are learning the fundamentals of sound creation. Pay particular attention to the *universal implications* of such sections as "Checking Out Functions," "The Tool Kit," "The Secrets," and "Ear Training."

★ You'll find that "Lesson Five: FM Synthesis" is directly applicable to any FM synthesizers, such as Yamaha's DX and TX series, as well as New England Digital's Synclavier. Much of the information in this lesson is unavailable from any other source.

★ If you own a synthesizer (or have access to one), make sure to experiment. Try out the examples, techniques, and concepts demonstrated in the course. More importantly, explore their implications!

Steve De Furia
Spring '86

About the Audio
on the tape . . .

Great pains were taken to keep the audio as clean and unprocessed as can be expected in this format. The synths were, in nearly all cases, taken direct into a **Harrison MR-3** 36 input audio console. The console was fed directly into a one-inch **Ampex** video machine. A 1/4" audio machine was also fed as a backup to the master video recorder. The monitors used were **Electro-Voice Sentry 100's.**

No compression or other processing was used aside from an **Eventide SP 2016** digital reverb unit. The SP 2016 was normally set on the "Room" setting for string sounds with about 30 to 40 milliseconds of pre-delay, and the decay varying between 0.6 and 2.5 seconds (depending on the articulation). For sounds other than strings, the "Hi-Density Plate" program was used with the same pre-delay and decay settings as above.

Each and every instrument was EQ'd at the console (some quite heavily, some less so), to approximate the sound (or sounds) normally heard on record. Some string sounds were slightly augmented by minimal use of both a room mic (a **Sennheiser 416M** shotgun), and a lapel mic (**Sony ECM 50**) worn by Steve. The lapel mic picked up part of the foldback signal, and in some cases, key clicks and other noises as well.

Table of Contents

SynthArts

SynthArts

LESSON ONE:
The Physics of Sound

What is Sound?

For the purposes of this course, we will define sound as disturbances capable of eliciting the sensation of hearing. (This means that the infamous tree that falls in the forest will definitely make a sound whether there is someone there to hear it or not.) This definition opens the door to more questions. How does sound travel from its starting point to our ears? We say that sound travels through the air, but what exactly is it that moves? The air? If that were so, we wouldn't need fans in the summertime, just a loud stereo. How do we hear? Are there limits to the loudest and softest sounds we can hear? The highest and lowest? What makes your voice sound different from everyone else's?

We perceive sounds as having three distinct attributes: **PITCH, TIMBRE** (tone color), and **LOUDNESS.** Musicians manipulate these three qualities of sound in order to produce melody, harmony, and rhythm. Synthesizers allow the sound designer to precisely manipulate these qualities in order to imitate or innovate sound events. In order to get the most out of a synthesizer, it is important to have a thorough understanding of the physical nature of sound and our subjective perception of it.

Observations

Let's start our exploration of sound by observing one of the oldest and simplest ways of making a musical sound, with a tightly stretched string. When the string is pulled and released, it is possible to note the following clues:

The string moves back and forth for some time after it is released. While it is moving, we hear a pitched sound with a definite tone color and loudness.

The sound becomes softer and softer over time. When the string stops, the sound stops.

The loudness of the sound seems to be related to how far the string is pulled before it is let go.

The pitch and timbre we hear remain constant, even when the sound's loudness changes.

Changing the tightness of the string changes its pitch but not its loudness or tone color.

The string is moving too fast for us to see clearly. As the sound fades away, the rate of the string's motion does not slow down.

These clues indicate that sound is linked to motion, or more to the point, pitched sound is linked to vibration. The *"Big Three" (pitch, timbre, and loudness)* seem to be independent of one another. Furthermore, there seems to be a connection between the way the string moves and how it sounds. Loudness is relative to how far the string is pulled. Pitch is relative to how tightly it is stretched. The timbre remains constant.

Investigating the physics behind this vibrating string will allow us to name and identify the parameters of sound responsible for pitch, timbre, and loudness. That, of course, is the first step to creating sounds. Don't be put-off by the word "physics." It simply means the study of the interactions between energy and matter, in this case — forces moving a mass, or, motion.

Vibrations

What's so unique about a taut string? Why is it particularly useful for making musical sounds? There are two reasons:

The sounds produced by a stretched string have a definite pitch that can be altered by changing tension on the string.

The sound coming from the string can easily be made to start, stop, and continue.

The string exhibits these musical properties because of a near perfect balance of forces. The tension on the string that holds it in a neutral, or equilibrium position, is called **restoring force.** When the string is stretched, the restoring force acts to pull the string back to this original position.

The distance the string is stretched is called **displacement.** The restoring force becomes greater as the displacement is increased. In other words, more and more force must be used to pull the string farther and farther from its neutral position. When the string is released, the restoring force will pull the string back towards its original position.

What makes a vibrating string unique is that the displacing force and the restoring force are exactly equal to each other. Since these two forces perfectly counteract each other, the time it takes the string to snap back to its original position will always be the same no matter how far it is displaced before it is let go.

Once the string is set in motion, its own momentum will keep it from stopping at the equilibrium position; and it will be displaced in the opposite direction of the original pull. The string will continue moving in this direction until the restoring force overcomes the momentum and pulls the string back towards the equilibrium position again.

VIBRATIONS

Get the picture? The interaction between restoring force, displacement, and momentum causes a cycle of motion called **periodic vibration.** This cycle would repeat forever if it weren't for things like air resistance and friction that "steal" energy from the system. Because the loss of energy is slight, the vibration continues for quite some time. With each swing the string covers a little less distance; but, since we have a balance of forces, each swing takes exactly the same amount of time to complete.

The motion of a single point on the string as it moves through one cycle of motion would look like FIG. 1.

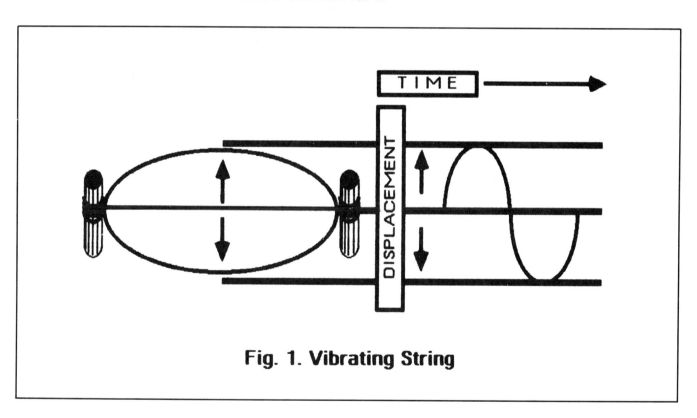

Fig. 1. Vibrating String

Wave Parameters

Any periodic vibration can be represented with the kinds of graphs shown in FIG. 2. These curves are called **waves.** They depict the pattern of motion of one cycle of vibration. Horizontal distance on such a graph represents the passage of time. Things on the right side of the graph happen after things on the left side. Vertical distance from the center line of the graph shows displacement (how far from the equilibrium position a vibrating object is at any given moment in time).

The general term for a wave's pattern of motion is **waveshape** or **waveform.** Waves with distinct geometric shapes are often referred to by the geometry of their waveshapes. The most common geometric waves are **square, triangle, sawtooth,** and **sine** waves. You have probably seen these shapes on the front panel graphics of many synthesizers. Not all waves are geometric. We will find that geometric waves have certain useful musical properties.

The highest and lowest points of the wave are called **peaks.** The vertical distance between two peaks is called **amplitude.**

One single pattern is called a **cycle** or **period.** The horizontal distance covered by one cycle is the **wavelength.** Often wavelength is expressed as how many cycles occur within a fixed amount of time. This is called **frequency.**

Frequency is often expressed as the number of cycles per second. The common unit of this measurement of time is **Hertz.** One Hertz (abbreviated Hz), is equal to one cycle per second. **kiloHertz,** or

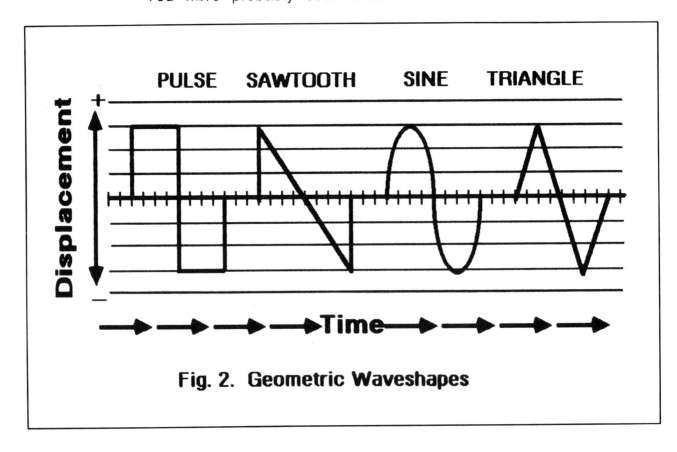

Fig. 2. Geometric Waveshapes

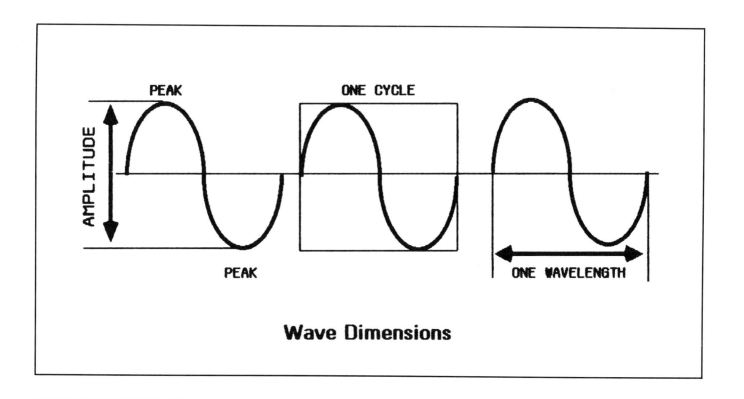

Wave Dimensions

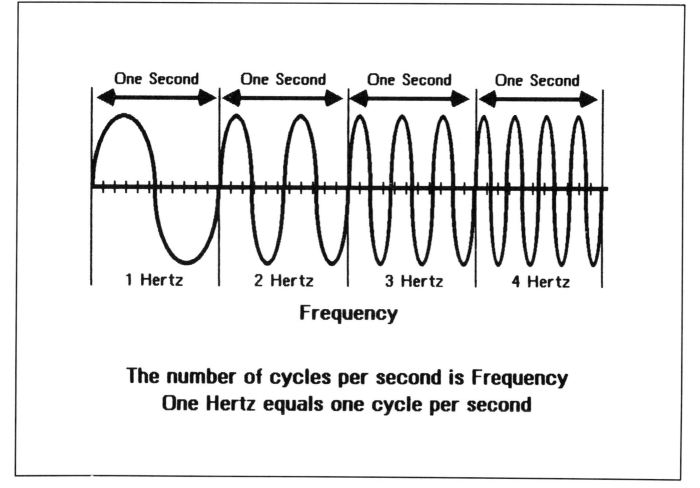

Frequency

The number of cycles per second is Frequency
One Hertz equals one cycle per second

WAVE PARAMETERS

kHz, is used to indicate thousands of cycles per second.

Waves, like sound, have three main parameters: *Frequency, Waveshape,* and *Amplitude.* These parameters are independent of each other. Changing a wave's amplitude does not change its shape or frequency. Changing frequency doesn't change shape or amplitude, and changing amplitude will not alter shape or frequency.

Now it is possible to equate aspects of a wave with specific aspects of the string's motion. **Amplitude** is equivalent to how far a string is pulled from its at-rest position, in other words, **displacement.** One complete vibration of the string is a **period** or **cycle.** The **rate** that the string vibrates is **frequency.** The **pattern** of the string's overall motion is called **waveshape.** For now, we will consider the string's waveshape to be a sine wave.

Great! Now that we have names, the string's motion is very easy to describe. As the string vibrates, its frequency and waveshape are constant. Its amplitude decreases continuously. Hmmm, three parameters of sound — three parameters of waves. Is it possible that they can be related to each other in some way? Of course they are!

We will see that altering a wave's frequency, waveshape, or amplitude will alter our perception of a sound's pitch, timbre, or loudness. But wait a minute, we can't talk about what we hear until we know how sound travels from the string to our ears.

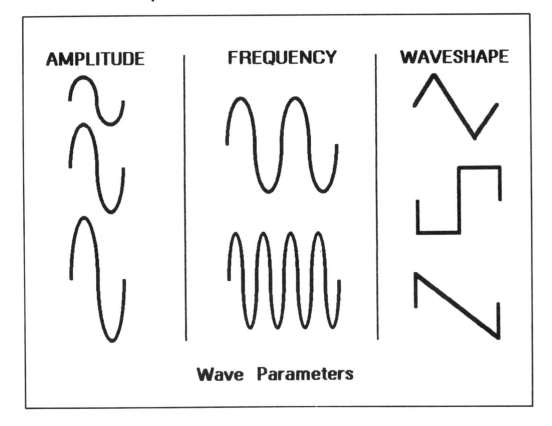

AMPLITUDE   **FREQUENCY**   **WAVESHAPE**

Wave Parameters

Propagation

From our observations it is safe to say that sound is "coming from" the string, but since we don't have to be physically touching the string to hear it, sound must somehow be "transmitted" through the air between the source and the observer. What is it that stimulates our sense of hearing, and how is it related to the vibrating string?

We know now that the string vibrates with a wavelike motion. It is, in fact, possible for waves to travel, but what exactly travels? The string obviously doesn't travel through the air to our ears. The air itself doesn't travel, if it did, making sounds would create breezes (giving a whole new meaning to "long-winded"). A traveling wave is actually a *disturbance* that moves through a substance. The substance itself doesn't travel. Does this seem a little hard to follow? It's really quite simple . . .

Imagine you are relaxing on a raft in the middle of a perfectly still pool at the Holiday Inn. "Heavy Mental," the local leather & metal band, is playing in the lounge. During a break, Naff Punter, the keyboardist gets involved in a discussion with the drummer, Slam Dunk, and Jonnie Velcro, the guitarist, about his relative merits as both a musician and poker player. The discussion concludes when Slam and Jonnie come out and throw Naff's aging "Poly-Kluge 2000" synthesizer into the pool.

The synth hits the water, sends waves out in all directions, and sinks like a ton of bricks. When the waves reach your raft, you feel ripples that move underneath you, traveling the length of the raft. What moved past you? No, it wasn't the water. If it were, the raft would have been swept away in the direction of the ripples, and you'd have bumped your head into the wall opposite a very distraught Naff, spilling your Pina Colada.

What moved past you was a disturbance (ripples) caused by the synthesizer displacing water when it was hurled into the pool. The disturbance moves, not the substance it is traveling through.

PROPAGATION

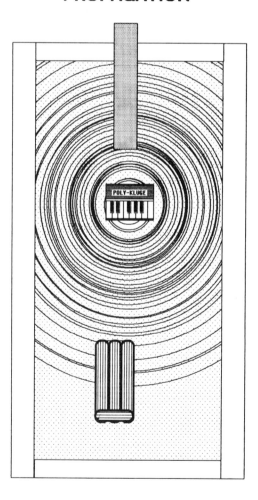

Synth Arts

PROPAGATION

We live within a sea of air. We hear the string because, like Naff's synth, it creates a disturbance that travels outwards in all directions from it. The traveling disturbance is called a **sound wave.** Unlike water waves, we cannot see sound waves directly; and that makes it difficult to tell what kind of disturbance is traveling through the air. However, we do know enough physics now to figure it out.

The string vibrates because of a balance of displacement and restoring forces. The transmission of sound waves through the air is based on the same principles.

The air around us is at a constant pressure. All of the molecules are equally spaced from each other. If the molecules are squeezed closer together or stretched farther apart, a restoring force will return them to their original spacing (pressure) when the source of compression or expansion is removed. Sound familiar?

When the string is displaced, it also displaces the air molecules around it, squeezing them close together, raising the pressure. Restoring force expands these molecules, returning them to their original pressure. However, this expansion pushes the neighboring molecules of air closer together; and restoring force expands them and so on, and so on. A kind of chain reaction occurs resulting in an area of higher than normal pressure that moves outwards from the string.

Meanwhile, the string has swung the other way. This time, instead of pushing molecules closer together, it pulls them further apart, lowering the pressure. Again, restoring force acts to return the pressure to normal by pulling the molecules closer together. This compression pulls the neighboring molecules of air further apart; and restoring force compresses them and so on, and so on. Now an area of lower than normal pressure moves along behind the area of high pressure.

The transference of energy from neighbor to neighbor in this manner is called **propogation.** The disturbance caused by the wavelike motion of the string is propagated through the air, traveling outwards in all directions from the source. It is a wave of air pressure called a compression wave. That's all there is to it! Sound waves are compression waves. What we actually hear are back and forth (high to low) changes in air pressure.

If you want to be a real stickler about it, we don't hear the string at all. We hear the disturbance it creates in our environment. Our sense of hearing is directly stimulated by minute fluctuations of air pressure that are caused by the physical movements of vibrating bodies.

10

The "Big Three"

Now that we know what sound is, and how it is transmitted from a source to our ears, we can take a closer look at the three parameters of sound. The typical synthesizer provides the sound designer with numerous ways of manipulating these three parameters. A thorough understanding of our perception of them is just as important to a synthesist as a knowledge of scales, rhythm, and harmony is to other musicians.

Loudness

Our perception of loudness is directly related to the wave parameter, *amplitude.* A sound-wave, like all moving waves, is a form of energy. The amplitude of a wave is an indicator of how much power the wave contains at a given moment.

The power represented by a sound wave's amplitude is usually referred to as **intensity**. A distinction is made between intensity and loudness because our perception of changes in loudness is not linear with respect to the changes in intensity that cause them.

The softest sounds that we can hear occur at a loudness level called the **"Threshold of Sensation."** These sounds are very, very quiet. In fact, it is almost impossible to find an environment where it is quiet enough to experience this level of loudness. There are special rooms that have been designed to be absolutely silent and totally sound proof. In such a room it is possible to hear the blood rushing through the vessels in your inner ear. This would be the loudness level of the *"Threshold of Sensation."* We will refer to this loudness level as **Ultra-Pianissimo**.

The loudest sounds occur at a point referred to as the **"Threshold of Feeling."** This is where sounds become so loud that they cause pain and are felt rather than heard. If you've ever been looking under the hood of a car when someone hit the horn, you know how loud this is. We will call this degree of loudness **Mega-Forte**.

"THE BIG THREE"

FIG. 3 shows this range from the softest to the loudest on two different scales. The intensity scale shows the range of power needed to produce sounds from the threshold of sensation to the threshold of feeling. The units of measurement show the relative amounts of power needed to produce different intensities.

The loudness scale shows this range as the difference in perceived loudness from the softest sound (Ultra Pianissimo) to the loudest (Mega-Forte). The units of measurement on this scale show the relative difference in loudness between these sounds.

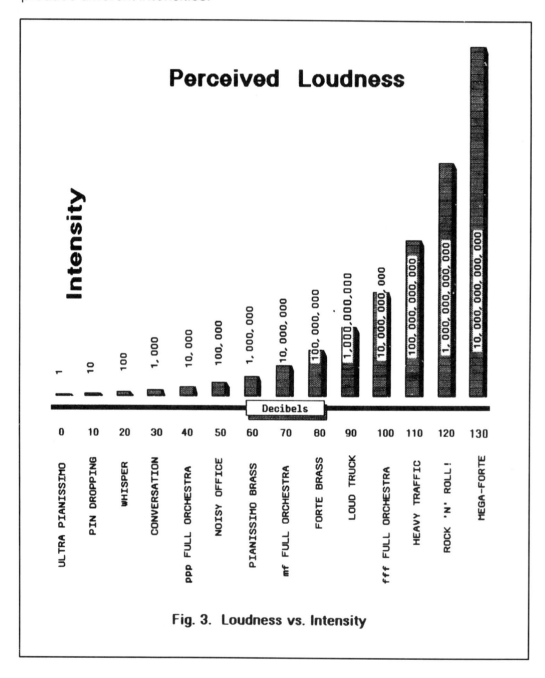

Fig. 3. Loudness vs. Intensity

"THE BIG THREE"

What is the difference in power between the highest and lowest intensities? What is the difference in loudness between the softest and loudest sounds? Let's look at the power involved first.

A common measurement of power that we are all familiar with is the **Watt.** We associate it with the brightness of light bulbs and the loudness of amplifiers. Think for a second about how much energy is used to produce the light from a 100 Watt bulb. Now try to imagine how much LESS power is used to produce the light from a single LED (like those you find on almost any synthesizer panel). An LED uses about one tenth of one watt. The difference in power between the 100 watt bulb and the LED is about 1000 to 1. The power in the loudest sounds we can hear is about one thousandth of one watt (when measured at the surface of the ear), 100 times LESS power than the LED (and that's for the loudest sounds). What do you think the difference in power is between that and the softest sounds we can experience? 100 to 1? 1,000 to 1? 1,000,000 to 1?

The softest sound that humans can perceive is produced by a power of *one tenth of one quadrillionth of one watt!* That's a decimal point followed by *fifteen* zeroes and then a one (.0000000000000001 watts). This represents an overall ratio of intensity of *ten billion* to one between the loudest and softest sounds we can hear! To show the same power difference from the LED we would need a *one billion watt bulb!*

This power ratio between loudest and softest sounds is deceptive, however. We certainly don't think of volume changes in these enormous quantities. We don't say "Could you play that a couple of million times louder please?" or, "Yo — Buddy! Would you mind turning that thing down a few billion notches or so?"

Our response to Intensity change is not linear. It takes ever increasing amounts of power to produce what we hear as equal changes in volume. In fact, we hear only an apparent doubling of loudness every time the power involved is multiplied by ten. That means we need *ten times the power* every time we want to be *twice as loud.* Furthermore, the softest sound could be doubled in apparent loudness only thirteen times before it reached the Threshold of Feeling.

There is a loudness scale called the **decibel (dB)** scale that compensates for the non-linearity of our loudness perception. Every change of 10 dB represents an increase or decrease in loudness by a factor of two, and in intensity by a factor of ten. The dynamic range of a symphony orchestra from silence to "triple forte" is in excess of 100 dB.

Our ability to hear relative changes in loudness is not very refined. A relative change of 1 decibel is about the smallest difference we can hear.

"THE BIG THREE"

Pitch

The wave parameter **frequency** is associated with our perception of pitch. As with loudness perception, there are definite upper and lower limits to pitch perception. The "lower threshold of pitch" is generally agreed to be 20 Hz (20 times a second), while the "upper threshold of pitch" is accepted to be 20,000 Hz.

We do not hear pitch changes in a linear manner relative to frequency changes. The basic pitch unit for the musician is the octave. Concert A is often tuned to 440 Hz. An octave above this pitch is 880 Hz, the next

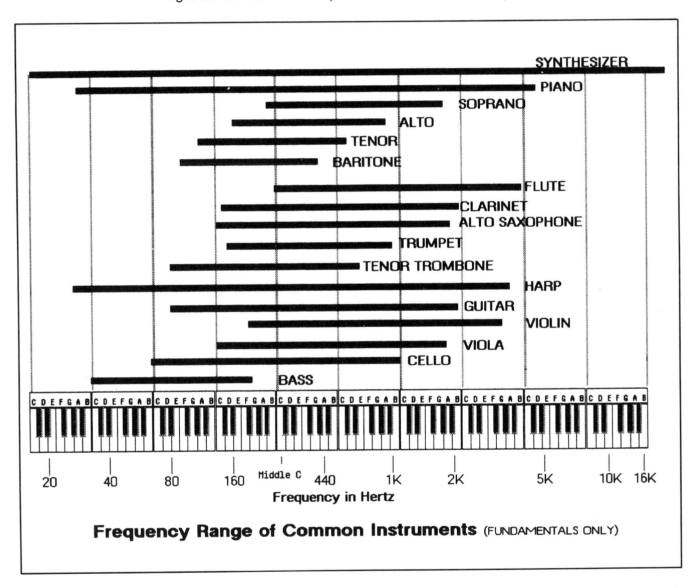

Frequency Range of Common Instruments (FUNDAMENTALS ONLY)

14

"THE BIG THREE"

octave higher is 1760 Hz. An octave below concert A would be 220 Hz and the next one below that, 110 Hz. If we listen to a pitch that changes from 110 Hz, to 220 Hz, to 440 Hz, to 880 Hz and so on, we would hear the pitch change in a linear fashion. The pitch would change by an interval of an octave each time. However, the frequency of each pitch changes by unequal amounts; it doubles for each octave of pitch change.

The octave is related to a frequency change of 2/1. Multiplying a frequency times two will shift the pitch up one octave, and dividing it by two will shift it down one octave. Pitch intervals are often expressed as ratios since it is the relative, not the numerical, difference between two frequencies that determine the pitch change we hear. For example, the pitch interval of a fifth can be expressed as a frequency ratio of 3/2, a fourth as 4/3.

The common scale in use today is the **tempered scale.** It divides the octave into 12 equal intervals called **tempered semitones.** Each key on a standard keyboard has a frequency that is 1.05946 times higher than the key immediately below it. Multiplying one by 1.05946 twelve times (once for each semitone in an octave) gives you two, which coincides with the octave ratio of 2/1.

A semitone can be divided into equal units called cents. A cent is 1/100th of a semitone. An octave, therefore, would be 1200 cents. A quartertone would be 50 cents.

There are *ten octaves* between the highest and lowest pitches that can be heard. We are much more sensitive to discrete changes in frequency than we are to changes in intensity. Virtually anyone can hear the difference between two adjacent steps on the semitone scale. On the

average, most people can hear differences as slight as *4 cents* (0.04 of one semitone.) This is a remarkable ability, especially when compared with our lesser ability of discriminating between different loudness levels.

Timbre

The parameter **waveshape** is directly related to our perception of **timbre,** or **tone color.** While both loudness and pitch are quantitative (they have definite limits and can be measured in units), timbre is qualitative. There is no limit to timbre perception because there is no limit to the number of possible waveshapes. Every different waveshape has a distinct tone quality. Different musical instruments produce sounds with different waveshapes. This is the reason an A-flat on a trumpet sounds different than the same A-flat played on a guitar.

It is hard to tell simply by looking at a wave's shape what its timbre will be like. In general, the more complicated the shape, the richer the tone color. The simplest shape is a sine wave. It has a pure, dull timbre. A tuning fork produces such a timbre.

With a few exceptions, most sources of sound produce waves that are considerably more complex than sine waves. Remember, waveshape is the pattern of a vibrating object's motion. A complex waveshape represents a complex vibration. Most sources of sound are actually vibrating at several different frequencies and amplitudes simultaneously. These individual vibrations combine to form the wave's overall shape. Since each of these vibrations is only a part of the

"THE BIG THREE"

overall waveform, they are called **partials.** Each partial is itself a simple vibration; i.e. a sine wave.

How can two or more simple vibrations combine to form one complex shape? . . .

Train #1

Imagine you are on a train platform with a can of spray paint in your hand (Don't worry, it's OK to be an imaginary vandal). As a train speeds by, you repeatedly move your arm up and down spraying the side of the train. If your motion is at a constant speed, you will have painted a sine wave across the side of the cars. One simple vibration produces a sine wave.

As the next train passes the platform, you start painting again; but this time (unknown to you) a transit cop comes up from behind, grabs you, and shakes you up and down as you are shaking the can of paint up

and down. He is quite agitated and is shaking you faster than you are shaking the can (He must be pretty upset; he's moving you twice as fast as you are moving the spray can). However, you weigh more than the can does, so he can't move you up and down as far as you can move the spray. Now we have two simple vibrations: yours and the transit cop's. Each one is individually a sine wave, each with its own frequency and amplitude. Both vibrations are occuring simultaneously. The pattern sprayed on the side of the train will be a new shape this time.

Train #2

"THE BIG THREE"

Looking at even such a relatively simple waveshape as this one, it is hard to tell from shape alone what individual partial frequencies and amplitudes were combined to form it. A **spectrum plot** is another way of graphing waveshape. Instead of showing amplitude changes over time, it shows amplitude over frequency.

Each vertical bar represents one partial (a single sine wave). The height of the bar shows its amplitude. Its horizontal placement on the graph shows its relative frequency.

A spectrum plot of the wave you painted on the first train would have a single bar that represented your movement of the spray can. A spectrum plot of grafitti on the second train would have two bars. One for you and one for the transit cop. The cop's partial would be shown as having twice the frequency and less amplitude than your partial.

The number of partials, and their relative frequencies and amplitudes, will determine the tone color of a sound. In general, the more partials in a wave the brighter the timbre. The frequency that corresponds to one complete cycle of the wave is called the **fundamental frequency.** It is this frequency that we perceive as a waveform's pitch.

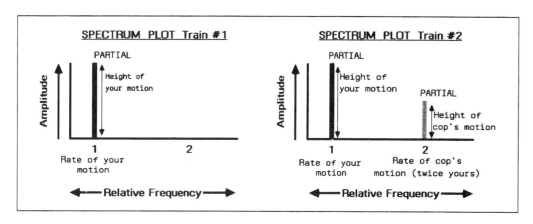

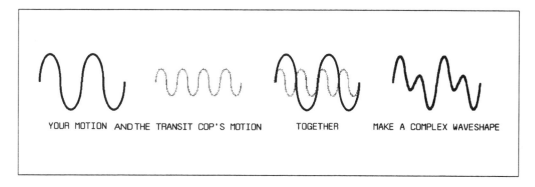

"THE BIG THREE"

Periodic vibrations, ones whose waveshape remains constant, contain partials that are related in a simple way. Their frequencies are 2, 3, 4 (and so on), times the fundamental's frequency. This series of pitch intervals is called the **harmonic series.** All geometric waveshapes have partial structures that are made up of some combination of the harmonic series. (FIG. 4)

FIGS. 5-8 compare the partial structure of sine, sawtooth, square and triangle waves.

Not all sounds have only partials at the harmonic frequencies. FIGS. 9-12 compare the partial structure of several musical sources of sound. Lessons One, Two, and Five contain several computer animations that will let you see, and hear, the timbre changes that result when the partial structure of a sound's spectrum is altered.

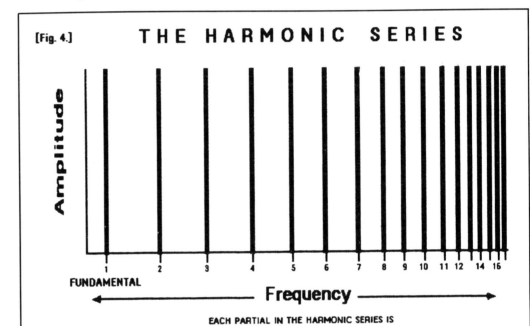

[Fig. 4.] THE HARMONIC SERIES

EACH PARTIAL IN THE HARMONIC SERIES IS
A WHOLE NUMBER MULTIPLE OF THE FUNDAMENTAL FREQUENCY

PARTIAL	FREQUENCY in HERTZ	RATIO to FUNDAMENTAL	INTERVAL from Fundamental OCTAVES – SEMITONES.CENTS
FUNDAMENTAL	110	1	UNISON
TWO	220	2	1–0
THREE	330	3	1–7.02
FOUR	440	4	2–0
FIVE	550	5	2–3.86
SIX	660	6	2–7.02
SEVEN	770	7	2–9.69
EIGHT	880	8	3–0
NINE	990	9	3–2.04
TEN	1100	10	3–3.86
ELEVEN	1210	11	3–5.51
TWELVE	1320	12	3–7.02
THIRTEEN	1430	13	3–8.40
FOURTEEN	1540	14	3–9.68
FIFTEEN	1650	15	3–10.88
SIXTEEN	1760	16	4–0

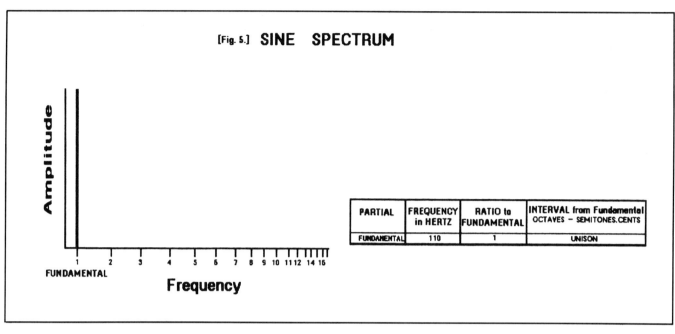

[Fig. 5.] **SINE SPECTRUM**

PARTIAL	FREQUENCY in HERTZ	RATIO to FUNDAMENTAL	INTERVAL from Fundamental OCTAVES — SEMITONES.CENTS
FUNDAMENTAL	110	1	UNISON

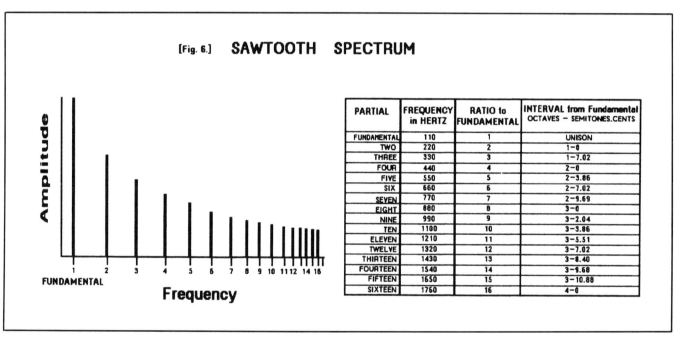

[Fig. 6.] **SAWTOOTH SPECTRUM**

PARTIAL	FREQUENCY in HERTZ	RATIO to FUNDAMENTAL	INTERVAL from Fundamental OCTAVES — SEMITONES.CENTS
FUNDAMENTAL	110	1	UNISON
TWO	220	2	1—0
THREE	330	3	1—7.02
FOUR	440	4	2—0
FIVE	550	5	2—3.86
SIX	660	6	2—7.02
SEVEN	770	7	2—9.69
EIGHT	880	8	3—0
NINE	990	9	3—2.04
TEN	1100	10	3—3.86
ELEVEN	1210	11	3—5.51
TWELVE	1320	12	3—7.02
THIRTEEN	1430	13	3—8.40
FOURTEEN	1540	14	3—9.68
FIFTEEN	1650	15	3—10.88
SIXTEEN	1760	16	4—0

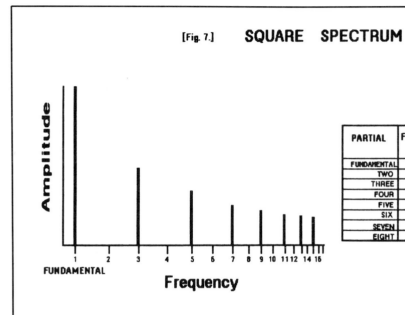

[Fig. 7.] SQUARE SPECTRUM

PARTIAL	FREQUENCY in HERTZ	RATIO to FUNDAMENTAL	INTERVAL from Fundamental OCTAVES — SEMITONES.CENTS
FUNDAMENTAL	110	1	UNISON
TWO	330	3	1—7.02
THREE	550	5	2—3.86
FOUR	770	7	2—9.69
FIVE	990	9	3—2.04
SIX	1210	11	3—5.51
SEVEN	1430	13	3—8.40
EIGHT	1650	15	3—10.88

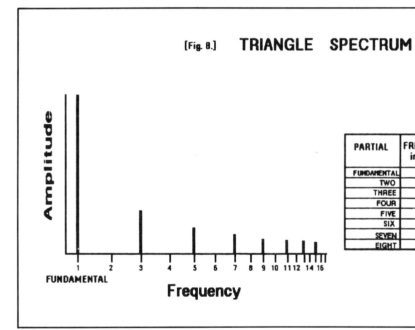

[Fig. 8.] TRIANGLE SPECTRUM

PARTIAL	FREQUENCY in HERTZ	RATIO to FUNDAMENTAL	INTERVAL from Fundamental OCTAVES — SEMITONES.CENTS
FUNDAMENTAL	110	1	UNISON
TWO	330	3	1—7.02
THREE	550	5	2—3.86
FOUR	770	7	2—9.69
FIVE	990	9	3—2.04
SIX	1210	11	3—5.51
SEVEN	1430	13	3—8.40
EIGHT	1650	15	3—10.88

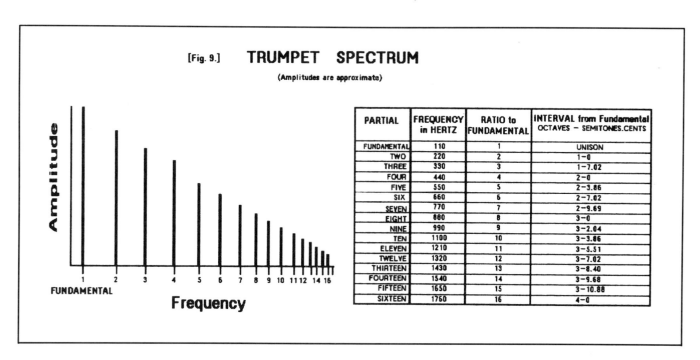

[Fig. 9.] **TRUMPET SPECTRUM**

(Amplitudes are approximate)

PARTIAL	FREQUENCY in HERTZ	RATIO to FUNDAMENTAL	INTERVAL from Fundamental OCTAVES – SEMITONES.CENTS
FUNDAMENTAL	110	1	UNISON
TWO	220	2	1–0
THREE	330	3	1–7.02
FOUR	440	4	2–0
FIVE	550	5	2–3.86
SIX	660	6	2–7.02
SEVEN	770	7	2–9.69
EIGHT	880	8	3–0
NINE	990	9	3–2.04
TEN	1100	10	3–3.86
ELEVEN	1210	11	3–5.51
TWELVE	1320	12	3–7.02
THIRTEEN	1430	13	3–8.40
FOURTEEN	1540	14	3–9.68
FIFTEEN	1650	15	3–10.88
SIXTEEN	1760	16	4–0

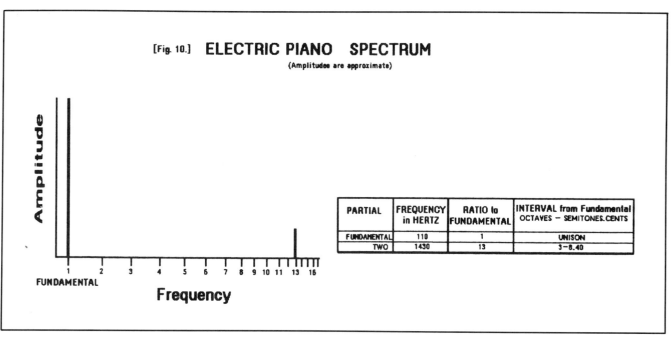

[Fig. 10.] **ELECTRIC PIANO SPECTRUM**

(Amplitudes are approximate)

PARTIAL	FREQUENCY in HERTZ	RATIO to FUNDAMENTAL	INTERVAL from Fundamental OCTAVES – SEMITONES.CENTS
FUNDAMENTAL	110	1	UNISON
TWO	1430	13	3–8.40

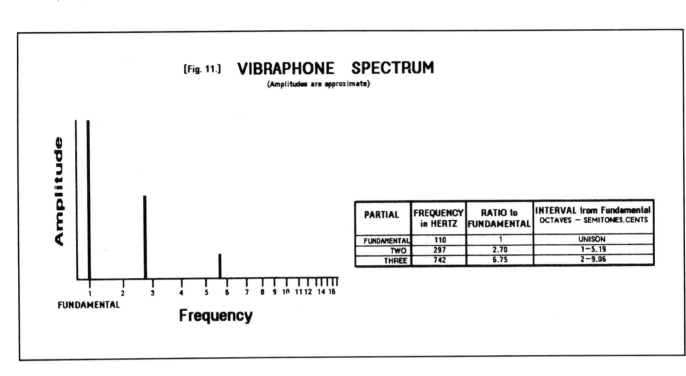

[Fig. 11.] **VIBRAPHONE SPECTRUM**
(Amplitudes are approximate)

PARTIAL	FREQUENCY in HERTZ	RATIO to FUNDAMENTAL	INTERVAL from Fundamental OCTAVES — SEMITONES.CENTS
FUNDAMENTAL	110	1	UNISON
TWO	297	2.70	1−5.19
THREE	742	6.75	2−9.06

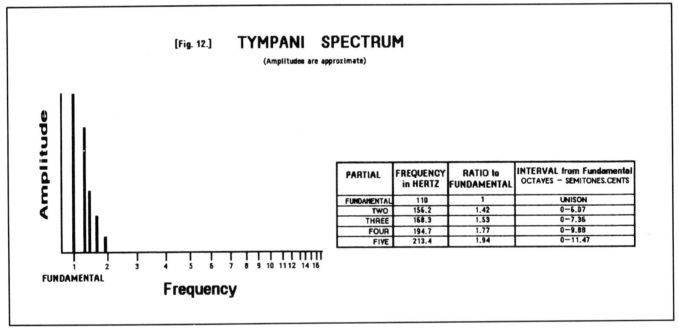

[Fig. 12.] **TYMPANI SPECTRUM**
(Amplitudes are approximate)

PARTIAL	FREQUENCY in HERTZ	RATIO to FUNDAMENTAL	INTERVAL from Fundamental OCTAVES — SEMITONES.CENTS
FUNDAMENTAL	110	1	UNISON
TWO	156.2	1.42	0−6.07
THREE	168.3	1.53	0−7.36
FOUR	194.7	1.77	0−9.88
FIVE	213.4	1.94	0−11.47

Summing It All Up

Waves that originate at a vibrating source will be perceived as sound if they have both frequency and amplitudes that fall within the limits of human perception. The three parameters of sound: **pitch, timbre,** and **loudness** correspond to the three physical aspects of a wave's motion: **frequency, waveshape,** and *amplitude.*

The sensation of pitch is directly related to frequency. Frequencies between 20 and 20,000 Hertz are heard as pitches. Frequencies above this range are inaudible. Frequencies below it are rhythmns (they are heard as individual events). We are very sensitive to pitch changes. The average person can hear changes in pitch that are only thousandths of the overall range.

The sensation of loudness is directly related to a sound wave's amplitude. A sound's loudness is an indication of how much energy was required to produce it. The difference in energy between the loudest and softest sounds that we hear is enormous (10 billion to one). Our ability to hear changes in loudness is not very refined. The average person can discern no more than 130 equal loudness changes in this entire power range.

The quality of timbre is directly related to a wave's shape. There are no limits to timbre perception. Any sound that we can hear must, by definition, have a tone color. Most sounds are caused by complex vibrations. They are made up of many individual components called partials. The partial structure of a wave is called a spectrum.

Any waveshape that repeats exactly from cycle to cycle will have partials whose frequencies belong to the harmonic series. Changing the partial structure of a sound will change its timbre.

The parameters pitch, timbre, and loudness are mutually independent.

NOTES:

24

LESSON TWO:
Making Waves

Musical Instruments

All musical instruments have certain things in common. Whether it is acoustic or electronic, analog or digital, a musical instrument must allow the musician to perform precise alterations of pitch, timbre, and loudness. This is, after all, the essence of musical expression.

Sources, Modifiers and Controllers

Any musical instrument can be broken down into three main areas, each with its own function.

▶ **SOURCES:** Each instrument has at least one source of sound (some type of vibrating body that is set in motion by the player). It may be a taut string, a bamboo reed, a stretched skin, a column of air, or some other vibrating object. These are called sources and are responsible for the basic waveshape produced by an instrument.

▶ **MODIFIERS:** Modifiers alter a source's waveshape and amplitude. They make no sound by themselves, they can only alter timbre and/or loudness. A trumpet mute is a good example of a modifier. It makes no sound of its own, yet it dramatically alters both loudness and timbre of the trumpet's sound.

▶ **CONTROLLERS:** Controllers, like modifiers, make no sound themselves. Musicians use them to alter the "Big Three" in order to express musical ideas. A violin bow, piano keys and xylophone mallets are some examples of controllers.

A stretched string by itself does not make a musical instrument. True, as a source it does make a sound when plucked; but it's not very loud, has an uninteresting timbre, and can only play one pitch.

Stretching the string over a carefully designed wooden box, like the body of a violin changes everything. The violin's body acts as a modifier. It alters the original vibration of the string in two ways: it changes the amplitude making it louder, and it alters the string's basic spectrum giving it a more pleasing tone color. By pressing the string against the neck of the instrument, the player can shorten its length and therefore alter the sound's pitch. A bow is used to start, stop, and control the amplitude of the string's vibration. The fingers of the player, the neck, and bow are controllers. They allow the violinist to precisely perform changes in pitch, timbre, and loudness.

Music Machines

Ultimately every musical instrument is a mechanical device. Each is really a machine that has been specialized to provide the performer with various ways of instantaneously controlling a sound's frequency, waveshape, and amplitude.

A player must master a unique set of physical skills before it is possible to perform effectively on a particular instrument. These skills do not automatically translate from one type of instrument to another. A world class cellist will not be able to instantly play the marimba without first learning a new set of performance techniques.

It is possible to list the general skills of musical expression even though the physical techniques change with the type of instrument being played.

**MUSICAL
INSTRUMENTS**

▶ **Articulation:** The ability to control the duration of a sound's overall pitch, timbre, and loudness. This is the basic skill of stating a melody.

▶ **Dynamics:** The ability to articulate with smooth or abrupt changes in any, or all, of the "Big Three." Dynamics such as crescendos or pitch bends give life to the phrasing of melody.

▶ **Modulation:** The ability to periodically vary pitch, timbre, or loudness over the course of a single duration. Techniques such as vibrato and tremolo add character to the individual notes of a melody.

The physical construction of an instrument influences the playing style of the performer. Synthesizers are unique in that they can be configured in a variety of different ways, allowing the performer to emulate many different playing styles. In many cases it is not necessary to acquire a new set of physical skills for different styles of performance.

This is both a blessing and a curse. Since it is relatively easy for synthesists to simulate certain types of expression, very often they don't bother to concentrate on specific musical styles. The end results are, more often than not—bland, lifeless performances.

For this reason, we will find that the most important functions of any synthesizer are those that allow the player to control changes in pitch, timbre, and loudness. These are the functions which allow an individual to develop a *personal style of expression.*

Synthesizer Concepts

Unlike acoustic instruments, synthesizers have no vibrating source. They are incapable of creating sound waves unless they are connected to a loudspeaker of some sort. The synthesist is actually generating, modifying, and controlling electronic "vibrations" that must be converted into sound waves before they can be heard.

There are two different types of electronic circuits used in synthesizers: **analog** and **digital.** An analog circuit produces a continuously changing electrical signal.

Digital circuits use streams of numbers to represent changing values. These numbers are converted (with the assistance of a micro processor) into an electrical signal.

The terms **"analog synthesizer"** and **"digital synthesizer"** refer to the type of circuits used to produce and modify sounds. In this Lesson, and Lessons Three and Four, we will be looking primarily at analog synthesizers. In Lesson Five, we will concentrate on an instrument that is quite different; it uses digital circuits for sound production and modification. Virtually every synthesizer available today contains both analog and digital circuitry.

In either case, the final output of a synthesizer is an electronic signal. It is important to understand how electricity can be converted into sound waves. Oh, no! Does this mean a course in Electronics-101 before we can learn about synthesizers?

Electronics-101

Here's what we need to know about electronics:

> Electricity is the *bi-directional* flow of electrons.
> The *"pressure"* of the flow can be varied.

We don't care about what electrons are, or where they come from. All we care about is that they can be made to "move" in either of two directions, and the force of that movement is variable.

Electrons can flow in either a *positive* (+) or *negative* (-) direction. The measurement of the "pressure" exerted by the flow is called **voltage.**

When a speaker is connected to a source of electricity, a *positive voltage flow* will cause it to *push outwards* compressing the air around it creating an area of high pressure. A *negative voltage flow* will cause it to pull *inwards* expanding the air around it creating an area of low pressure.

These compression waves will be propagated through the air. If they occur with appropriate frequency, waveshape, and amplitude, a sound will be heard.

The flow of electrons through the speaker causes it to vibrate, creating sound waves. Synthesizers contain analog and/or digital circuits that

SYNTHESIZER CONCEPTS

generate voltage changes which can be thought of as a direct equivalent to a vibrating source of sound. Specifically, these circuits generate voltage waveforms whose frequency, waveshape, and amplitude can be changed in a variety of musically expressive ways.

Electronic signals that are meant to be converted into sound waves are referred to as **audio.** Believe it or not, that's all we need to know about electronics. In terms of sound waves — pressure, displacement, and voltage are all directly related to the wave parameter amplutide. Frequency always refers to the rate of change in amplitude. Waveshape always refers to the pattern of one cycle of amplitude change.

Block Diagramming Basics

There is a simple method of graphically showing the interconnections within a system called **block diagramming.** We will be using it to notate various synthesizer configurations. The beauty of block diagrams is that they can be translated from instrument to instrument regardless of the manufacturer or model.

Each box in a block diagram represents one, and only one, function. Any synthesizer will require a minimum of three blocks: source, modifier, and controller.

There are only two basic types of block diagram functions: **generators** and **processors.** A source is a generator. It is the origination of audio signals. Modifiers are processors. They alter audio signals but generate no signals by themselves. Controllers are also generators. They produce a type of signal called a **control signal.** We won't be looking at controllers until Lesson Three. For now, all we need to know about controllers is that their signals are not audio and will not be heard.

The blocks can be connected in different ways to show how to make different kinds of sounds. The interconnection of these functions is governed by some simple rules.

▶Audio signals flow from *left* to *right.* A source will always be to the left of its modifiers.

▶Outputs from generators are drawn as *horizontal arrows* leaving the right side of a source or controller.

▶Processor inputs are on the *left side* of a block.

▶Both processors and generators can have control inputs. These are shown on the *bottom* of a box.

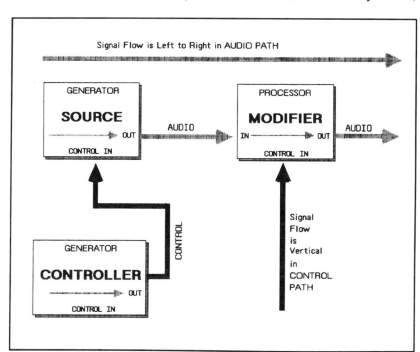

29

SYNTHESIZER CONCEPTS

There are two simple types of connections that can be made between blocks:

In a *processing pair,* the output of a generator is connected to the input of a processor.

In a *control pair,* the output of a generator is connected to the control input of either another generator or a processor.

Processing connections are drawn as horizontal (left to right) arrows.

Control connections are drawn as vertical (bottom to top) arrows.

For now, we are only concerned with diagramming the flow of audio signals. This is called the **audio path.** It can always be shown as a series of processing connections. The signal will always flow from left to right. A block diagram showing the audio path of an electric guitar connected to a wah-wah and a volume pedal would look like this. (FIG. 13)

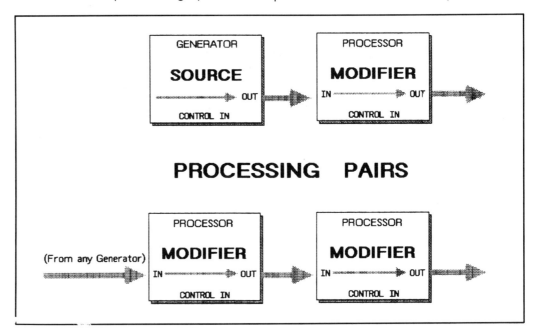

PROCESSING PAIRS

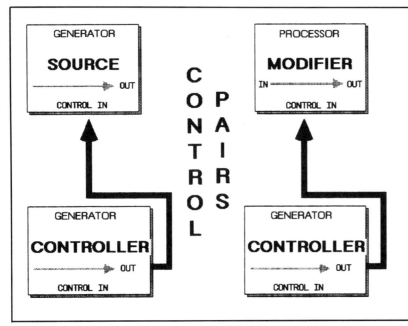

The guitar is the source. The wah-wah is a timbre modifier, and the volume pedal is a loudness modifier.

Virtually every analog synthesizer has an audio path that looks similar to FIG. 14.

The first step to understanding how to program these instruments is to learn about each individual function. In this lesson, we will concentrate on sources and modifiers. Lesson Three is about controllers and how to use them to create sounds. Block diagrams will be used as a reference to recreate these sounds on any synthesizer with similar functions.

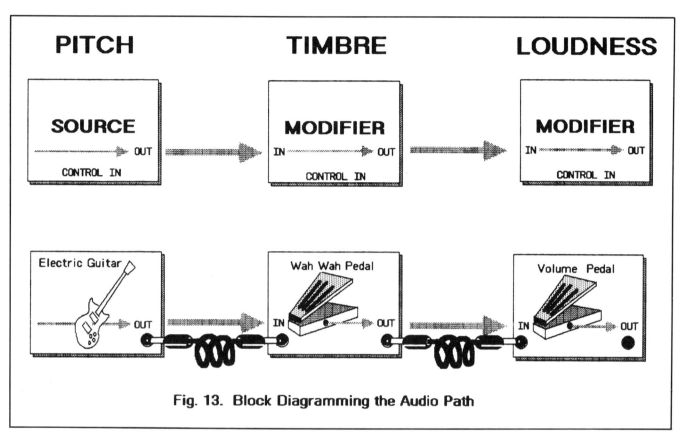

Fig. 13. Block Diagramming the Audio Path

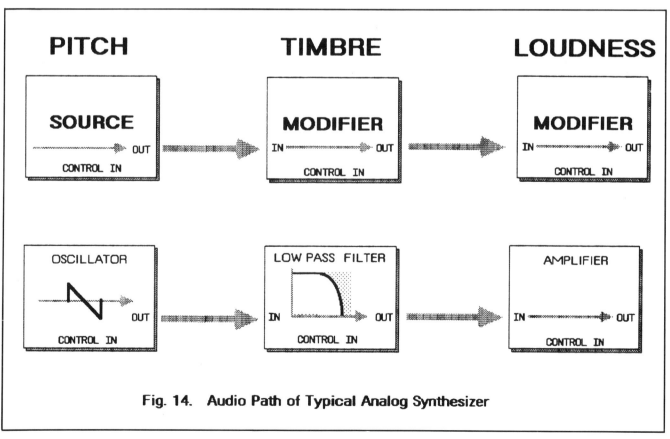

Fig. 14. Audio Path of Typical Analog Synthesizer

SYNTHESIZER CONCEPTS

Checking out Functions

Like the boxes in a block diagram, each synthesizer module has only one function. Although each module's function is different, they all. have certain things in common. In general, every major synthesizer function will have at least one variable parameter and/or one selectable feature. FIG. 15 shows the typical selectable features and variable parameters of common synthesizer functions.

Whenever you come across a new synthesizer, this simple check-out procedure will quickly orient you to the instrument's capabilities.

▶What if any, **selectable features** does the function have? These are generally associated with switches that allow you to choose "either/or," or "one of several," or "on/off."

▶Locate the function's **variable parameters.** Typically these are associated with manual controls like sliders, knobs or number ranges. They determine factors like "depth," "rate," and "more or less."

▶Find out if any of the function's variable parameters are **controllable** by other modules in the synthesizer.

▶Determine which of these features and parameters are **programmable.** Can their settings be memorized and recalled when you want to save a sound?

FUNCTION	SELECTABLE FEATURE	VARIABLE PARAMETER
Oscillator	Tuning Range Waveshape Sync	Frequency Pulse Width Level
Filter	Mode Roll—Off	Resonance Cut—Off Point
Amplifier	(NONE)	Output Level

32

SYNTHESIZER CONCEPTS

Synthesizer Sources

The **source** functions of a synthesizer can be thought of as providing the *raw materials* for sound design. The most common synthesizer source is the **oscillator** — sometimes called **VCO** or **DCO** (for Voltage Controlled Oscillator or Digitally Controlled Oscillator). The oscillator is the synthesizer function that generates the basic audio waveforms. Many synthesizers also have a second type of source called a **noise generator.**

In Lesson Two of the video tape, you will see and hear a complete demonstration of synthesizer sources.

Oscillators

The **oscillator** is the most useful source of audio waveforms on a synthesizer. It is responsible for a sound's pitch and basic spectrum (waveshape).

An oscillator will almost always have some kind of manual tuning control. Often there are both fine and coarse tuning controls. These controls are like the tuning pegs of a violin, they allow the player to adjust the overall pitch range of a sound. Some instruments also provide selectable tuning ranges, usually in octaves.

Common Functions

OSCILLATOR

SELECTABLE FEATURES

WAVEFORM :	
TUNING RANGE :	LO, 16', 8', 4', 2'
SYNC :	ON/OFF

VARIABLE PARAMETERS	[Common Control Sources]	CONTROL SOURCES
OUTPUT LEVEL	[1]	1 MANUAL
FREQUENCY	[1,2,3,4,5]	2 KEYBOARD
		3 BENDER
		4 LFO
PULSE WIDTH	[1,4,5]	5 ENVELOPE GENERATOR

SYNTHESIZER
CONCEPTS

Waveshapes

Most oscillators have more than one selectable waveshape, making it possible to choose between two or more basic timbres. The typical analog waveshapes are:

▶ **Sawtooth** — The sawtooth wave has partials at all of the harmonic frequencies. The amplitude of the partials changes relative to the fundamental's in the following manner. If the fundamental has an amplitude of 1, then the amplitude of the second partial is 1/2 that of the fundamental, the third partial 1/3, the fourth partial 1/4, and so on. Sawtooth waves have a bright brassy sounding timbre.

▶ **Square** — The square wave is a rectangular waveform with a spectrum containing only odd harmonic partials (harmonic partials 2, 4, 6, 8, etc., are missing). The relative amplitude of these partials change in a way similar to a sawtooth — 1, 1/3, 1/5, 1/7, 1/9, etc. The timbre of a square wave is less bright than a sawtooth and has a hollow "woody" sound.

▶ **Variable Pulse** — The variable pulse wave is a rectangular wave whose pulse width (see FIG. 16) can be altered. The partial structure of a pulse wave is determined by the *ratio* of the *pulse width* to the *rest of the wave.* For example: A square wave has a pulse width equal to 1/2 cycle and, as we have seen, every second harmonic partial is missing. A pulse wave with a pulse width of 1/3 cycle would be missing every third partial. A pulse width of 1/4 would have every fourth harmonic partial missing, etc. The relative amplitude of the partials changes in manner similar to that of a square or sawtooth wave. The timbre of a variable pulse wave will be dependent upon its pulse width. The dullest timbre is produced by a pulse width of 1/2 (square wave) as the width is made narrower or wider than this, the timbre will grow increasingly brighter. Very narrow (or very wide) pulse widths produce very bright, buzzy timbres.

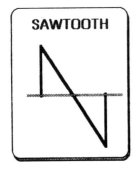

SAWTOOTH

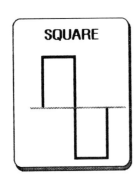

SQUARE

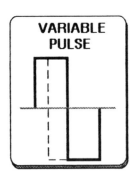

VARIABLE PULSE

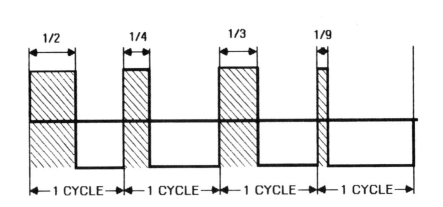

Fig. 16. PULSE WIDTH (or DUTY CYCLE) is the fraction of one cycle of a rectangular wave that is positive.

SYNTHESIZER CONCEPTS

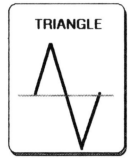

TRIANGLE

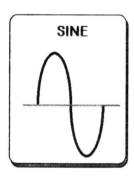

SINE

▶ **Triangle** — The triangle wave has a spectrum that, like the square wave, contains partials at only odd harmonic frequencies. The amplitude of these partials, relative to the fundamental's, changes in a more drastic manner than it does for sawtooth and square waves. The amplitude of the third harmonic partial is 1/9, the fifth 1/25, the seventh 1/49, etc. The timbre of the triangle wave is a hollow sound similar to a square wave. Since the partials are of much less amplitude than those of a square wave's, the triangle has a much duller sound.

▶ **Sine** — The sine wave is sometimes available as an audio waveform. It has no partials in its spectrum, only a fundamental. The timbre of a sine wave is pure and very dull.

With the exception of *pulse width,* the only parameter of any of these waveshapes that can be controlled by other synthesizer functions is *frequency.*

Sync

If an instrument has more than one oscillator, often one of them has a selectable feature called **SYNC** (because a pair of oscillators is required to take advantage of this feature). The output of one oscillator is used to control the frequency of the other in a special way. The controlling oscillator is referred to as the master, and the oscillator being controlled is called the slave. Sync forces the slave's tuning to a frequency that is exactly the same as the closest harmonic of the master's fundamental. If both oscillators were tuned fairly close to unison with each other, the slave will "lock in" to perfect tuning to the master frequency. As the slave's tuning is raised, it will jump to each successive harmonic frequency of the master's fundamental. It will still be possible to hear a slight amount of the fundamental frequency as well. This causes a timbre change rather than a pitch change when you listen to the slave's output. This is a unique sound and can be used for dramatic effect. It is demonstrated in Lessons Two and Four.

The main thing to remember about oscillators is that they allow the sound designer to choose a basic timbre and pitch range. The only thing you can control on most oscillators is frequency (for pitch changes) and pulse width (for timbre changes).

35

**SYNTHESIZER
CONCEPTS**

Noise
Generators

Radio static, wind, and running water are all sounds that are primarily unpitched in nature. The **noise generator** is the synthesizer's source of *unpitched* sound. Its partial structure changes in an unpredictable manner from instant to instant. The noise generator does not have any controllable parameters. Typically, the only parameter of a noise generator is loudness. On some instruments its output level is determined by the settings of a variable knob or slider. Some noise generators have just a simple On/Off level control.

Common Functions

NOISE GENERATOR *

SELECTABLE FEATURES

OUTPUT LEVEL: ON/OFF

VARIABLE PARAMETERS	[Common Control Sources]	CONTROL SOURCES
		1 MANUAL
OUTPUT LEVEL	[1]	

* On some NOISE GENERATORS, Output Level is <u>selectable</u>.
On others, it is <u>variable</u>.

SYNTHESIZER CONCEPTS

Source Mixing

In Lesson One, we learned that it is possible to create complex waveshapes by combining simple ones together (remember the cop and the spray paint?). The addition of different sources together is called **mixing.** Most synthesizers allow different source waveforms to be combined in various ways.

Wave Mixing

Some oscillators can output more than one waveform at once. This makes it possible to combine the spectrums of two waveshapes of exactly the same frequency, creating a new timbre.

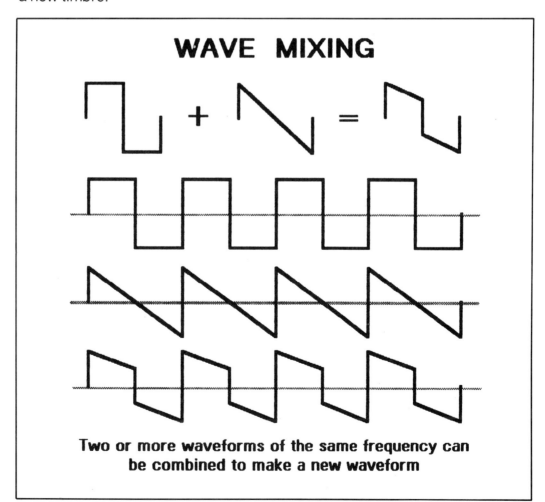

Two or more waveforms of the same frequency can be combined to make a new waveform

**SYNTHESIZER
CONCEPTS**

Chorus Effect

When the outputs of two (or more) oscillators are mixed together, it is possible to achieve what is called a **chorus effect.** This is the principle behind the **ensemble effect** demonstrated in Lesson Three.

The *difference* in frequency between the sources will have an effect on the resulting sound. If the interval between the sources is significant, a semi-tone or more, then each source will remain "independent" of the other. In other words, mixing a sawtooth and a square wave that were a perfect fifth apart, would result in a harmony. The pitches and timbres of each tone will be heard as being distinct from each other.

If the interval between the sources is small, less then a semi-tone, then a phenomenon called **chorusing** occurs. A steady loudness fluctuation, called **beating,** will be heard. The rate of the beats will equal the frequency difference between the two sources.

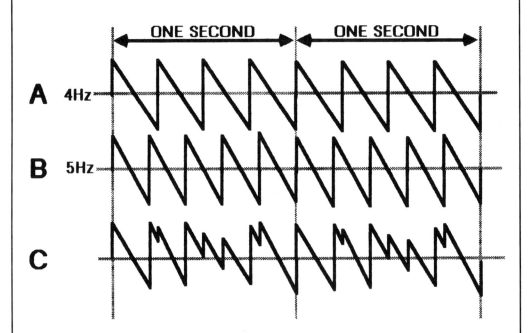

SOURCE MIXING

The complex pattern of wave C will repeat at a rate of 1 Hz.

This is equal to the difference in frequency of waves A and B (5Hz − 4Hz= 1Hz).

At audio frequencies this will be heard as "beating"

**SYNTHESIZER
CONCEPTS**

If one oscillator is tuned to A 440Hz, and another tuned slightly sharp to A 441Hz, the frequency difference between them is 1Hz. When these two oscillators are mixed together, the resulting sound will become louder and softer at a rate of once per second. If the tuning difference between them becomes greater, then the rate of the beating will increase.

This is a standard method of creating a "fat" sound with synthesizers (often called **detuning**). It is useful in simulating the sound of multiple instruments, and is most commonly used to emulate the sound of a string choir.

It is important to remember that the *rate* of beating is dependent on the *frequency difference* between the sources. Since frequency doubles for every pitch increase of an octave, the frequency difference between the sources will double as well.

$$440Hz \times 2 = 880Hz$$
$$441Hz \times 2 = 882Hz$$
$$882Hz - 880Hz = 2Hz$$

This means that as keys are played above the original tuning point, the beating will increase in rate.

One octave above the original pitch, the beating will be *twice* as fast. *Two octaves* above, the beating will be *four times* as fast! The beating will slow down as keys are played below the original tuning point. In other words, the rate of the chorus effect will change for every key played.

By no means is this undesirable. In fact, this is one of the most useful sound design tools available to the synthesist. If the initial detuning is set in the middle of the playing range, it is possible to minimize the total change in the chorusing rate.

The mixing sections of most synthesizers allow source waveforms to be combined at various amplitudes. These amplitude levels are usually programmable (they are stored with the "patch"), but they are not usually controllable by other synthesizer functions.

Synthesizer Modifiers

If synthesizer sources can be thought of as the raw materials of sound design, then **modifiers** are the basic tools used to *shape* these materials into finished sounds. Remember, modifiers make no sound themselves. They can only alter the parameters of a source's waveform.

Virtually every analog synthesizer has at least two modifiers. One alters a wave's amplitude for loudness changes. The other alters wave-shape for timbre changes.

Common Functions
AMPLIFIER

SELECTABLE FEATURES

(NONE)

VARIABLE PARAMETERS	[Common Control Sources]	CONTROL SOURCES
		1 MANUAL
OUTPUT LEVEL	[1,2,3]	2 ENVELOPE GENERATOR
		3 LFO

Amplifiers

The modifier used to change loudness is the **amplifier.** Typically, there are no selectable features associated with an amplifier. There is usually just one variable parameter, loudness (sometimes labeled gain, output level, or simply enough, volume). This variable parameter is always controllable with other synthesizer functions.

There is not much to say about amplifiers. They simply make a sound louder or softer by changing its amplitude. Most synthesizer amplifiers can only make the amplitude less than the original source's level. This kind of level change is called **attenuation** (which simply means: "to make less"). The typical amplifier can provide an overall loudness change of about 60 dB.

**SYNTHESIZER
CONCEPTS**

Filters

Filters are the standard timbre modifiers on all analog synthesizers. Timbre changes are probably the most distinctive qualities of musical sounds. Proper control of the filter is the most critical aspect of making almost any synthesizer sound.

There are several different types and variations of filters. However, they all work in the same basic way; and all have the same basic features.

Filters are really just sophisticated tone controls, like those found on a stereo or guitar amp. Like synthesizer amplifiers, they attentuate audio signals. Unlike amplifiers, this attenuation is *frequency dependent.* A filter can alter a wave's partial structure by selectively attenuating only certain frequencies. In other words, they can be used to "block out" certain partials while allowing others to pass unchanged. Since filters can only remove partials from a waveform, using them to make sounds is called **subtractive synthesis.**

Common Functions

FILTER

SELECTABLE FEATURES

MODE : LOW PASS   HIGH PASS   BAND PASS   BAND REJECT

ROLL—OFF :   12 dB/OCT (2 POLE)   24 dB/OCT (4 POLE)

VARIABLE PARAMETERS	[Common Control Sources]	CONTROL SOURCES
RESONANCE	[1]	1 MANUAL 2 KEYBOARD 3 ENVELOPE GENERATOR
CUT—OFF FREQUENCY	[1,2,3,4,5]	4 LFO 5 BENDER

Cut-Off Frequency

The frequency where this selective attenuation begins is called the **cut-off frequency** or **cut-off point.** Cut-off frequency is the main variable parameter of a filter. Control of this parameter is a fundamental skill for analog synthesists.

Frequencies on one side of the cut-off point will be attenuated, while frequencies on the other side will not be affected. The type of filter (called **mode**) will determine on *which side* of the cut-off point the attenuation occurs.

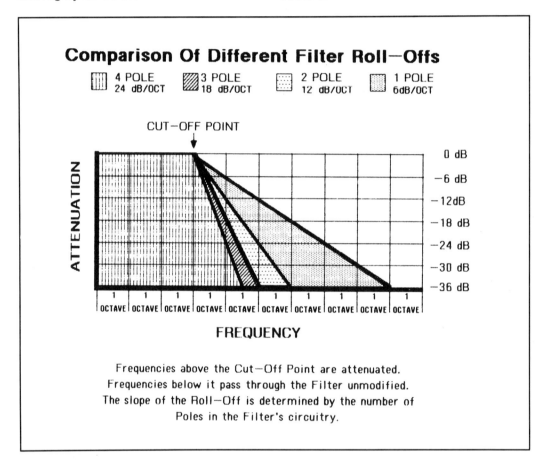

Comparison Of Different Filter Roll—Offs

4 POLE 24 dB/OCT   3 POLE 18 dB/OCT   2 POLE 12 dB/OCT   1 POLE 6dB/OCT

CUT—OFF POINT

ATTENUATION

0 dB
−6 dB
−12dB
−18 dB
−24 dB
−30 dB
−36 dB

OCTAVE OCTAVE OCTAVE OCTAVE OCTAVE OCTAVE OCTAVE OCTAVE OCTAVE OCTAVE

FREQUENCY

Frequencies above the Cut—Off Point are attenuated.
Frequencies below it pass through the Filter unmodified.
The slope of the Roll—Off is determined by the number of
Poles in the Filter's circuitry.

Roll-Off

The amount of attenuation will become *greater* as the interval distance beyond the cut-off point is increased. This attenuation curve is called *slope, or roll-off.* The amount of attenuation is usually measured in decibels, and the interval unit in octaves. **Steeper curves** will roll-off more decibels per octave.

There are particular component configurations within filter circuits called **poles.** The number of poles a filter has will determine how steep the roll-off is. Each pole will add 6dB per octave. A one pole filter has a roll-off of 6dB/Oct, two poles — 12dB/Oct, three poles — 18dB/Oct and four poles — 24dB/Oct. The

SYNTHESIZER CONCEPTS

most common filter is the four pole. Some synthesizers use two pole filters, and others have a selectable number of poles (usually 2 or 4). The more poles a filter has the fewer partials it will pass beyond its cut-off frequency. The "fat" sound of the original Mini-Moogs has been attributed to the fact that it was the first popular synthesizer with a four pole (24dB/Oct) filter.

Resonance

Another variable filter parameter is **resonance** (sometimes called **emphasis,** or **Q**). Resonance increases the amplitude of a band of frequencies near a filter's cut-off point, making them louder. As the resonance is turned up, this band becomes narrower and narrower. In the filter demonstration in Lesson Two, you will see how to use this feature to literally "focus in" the different partials of a source waveform.

On some filters, if the resonance control is turned up all the way, the filter will begin to emit a pitch. This is because the filter is literally "feeding back." If the filter's cut-off frequency is controllable from the keyboard, it is possible to use the filter as a source. In Lesson Three of this manual, there are some block diagrams that show you how to make use of this feature.

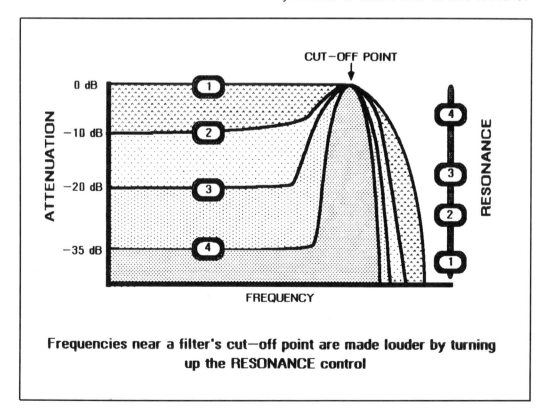

Frequencies near a filter's cut—off point are made louder by turning up the RESONANCE control

Low Pass Filter

Low pass filters attenuate frequencies *above* the cut-off point. This is the most useful filter mode because it changes a sources spectrum in a manner that is similar to the spectrum changes that occur in most musical instruments. When an oscillator is connected to the audio input of a low pass filter, nothing will be heard until the filter's cut-off frequency is raised to a point somewhere above the oscillator's fundamental frequency (this is demonstrated in Lesson Two). As the cut-off is raised, more and more of the wave's partials will pass through the filter. The sound will become brighter and brighter. The fundamental will always be present as long as any sound is passing through the filter.

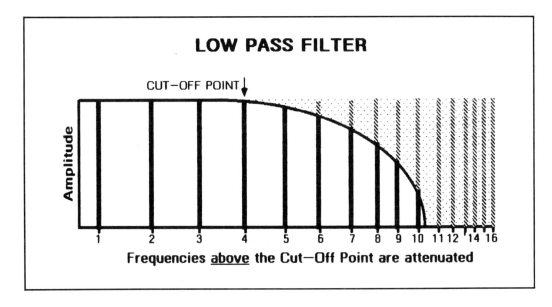

High Pass Filter

The **high pass filter** works in a manner exactly opposite that of the low pass. It will attenuate frequencies *below* the cut-off point. With a high pass filter, it is possible to remove the lower partials, including the fundamental, from a wave's spectrum creating a very thin timbre.

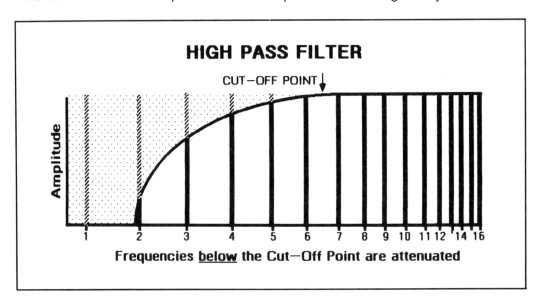

Band Pass Filter

The **band pass filter** removes frequencies *above and below* the cut-off point, allowing only a very narrow band of frequencies to pass through. This mode is very similar to a mid range EQ on a mixing console.

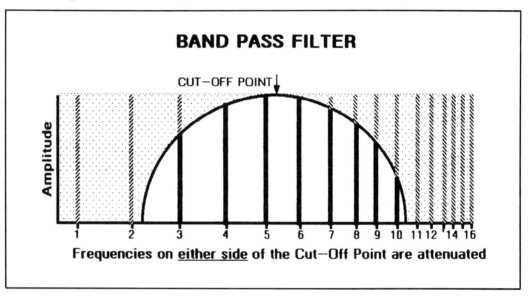

Notch Filter

The **notch filter** (sometimes called band reject) works in a manner exactly opposite from a band pass filter. It removes a narrow band of frequencies *at the filter's cut-off point* from a wave's spectrum.

All of the above filter modes are demonstrated in Lesson Two. Listen to the timbre changes thay make and watch the animations that show how these different types of filters effect the wave's partial structure. In Lesson Three, we will see how to use filters to simulate different kinds of instrumental tone production.

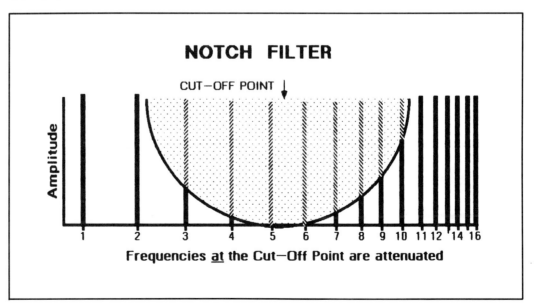

NOTES:

LESSON THREE:
The Sound Designer's Tool Kit

Musical Control

In order to express musical ideas, a musician must be able to control changes in the "Big Three." With acoustic instruments, he can accomplish these changes by manually controlling sources and modifiers. With synthesizers, the musician must learn both physical and automatic types of control of the parameters of sound.

The musician can directly manipulate the variable parameter settings of the different synthesizer sources and modifiers in order to articulate with dynamics and modulation. This can also be accomplished indirectly by using synthesizer functions called **controllers**. Controllers act like "robot hands." They will change parameters by remote control according to the way they are "programmed." A creative synthesist uses both types of controls for maximum musical effect.

The only controllable parameters on almost all analog synthesizers are:

▶**Pitch** — Oscillator frequency is the synthesizer parameter that when altered, produces a pitch change in a sound. Frequency can be raised or lowered, making a sound's pitch higher or lower.

▶**Timbre** — Filter cut-off point is the main parameter for timbre changes. The cut-off point can be raised or lowered, altering a wave's timbre by removing certain partials from its spectrum. In the case of a low pass filter, raising the cut-off point makes a sound brighter. This occurs because more and more partials above the fundamental will be heard. Lowering the cut-off point will make a sound darker. This happens because partials are removed from the spectrum until eventually only the fundamental will remain.

Increasing or decreasing an oscillator's **pulse width** will change timbre by adding or subtracting partials to a pulse wave's spectrum. This can change the hollow timbre of a square wave (pulse width 1/2), into a very bright, reedy timbre (pulse width very wide, or very narrow).

Another type of timbre change can be produced by raising or lowering the frequency of a sync oscillator. This will emphasize specific partials in the harmonic series.

▶**Loudness** — Amplifier output level is the synthesizer parameter associated with changes in loudness. Raising or lowering the output level will raise or lower a sound's loudness.

Control Concepts

There are usually no more than four basic parameters changing on an analog synthesizer at any time, no matter how sophisticated a sound is coming from the instrument.

Oscillator: Frequency and/or Pulse Width

Filter: Cut-Off Point

Amplifier: Output Level

In each case the type of change is the same. A parameter may be changed continuously through a range of values from low to high. One of the things that differentiates synthesizers from other instruments is the use of functions called controllers to produce these changes.

A controller is a function that generates an output with a variable amplitude. The amplitude of this control signal will change over time in various ways (depending on the particular control function). A controllable parameter will change from its initial setting, following the shape of the control signal's amplitude.

Block Diagramming

Unlike the audio path, which is fixed on most synthesizers, the control paths change from sound to sound. Block diagrams are very effective ways of showing the different critical connections between controllers and other synthesizer functions.

In a block diagram the connection between a controller and the device it is controlling is drawn as a vertical arrow. Often the output of one controller is routed to more than one function. For example, the keyboard is connected to each oscillator.

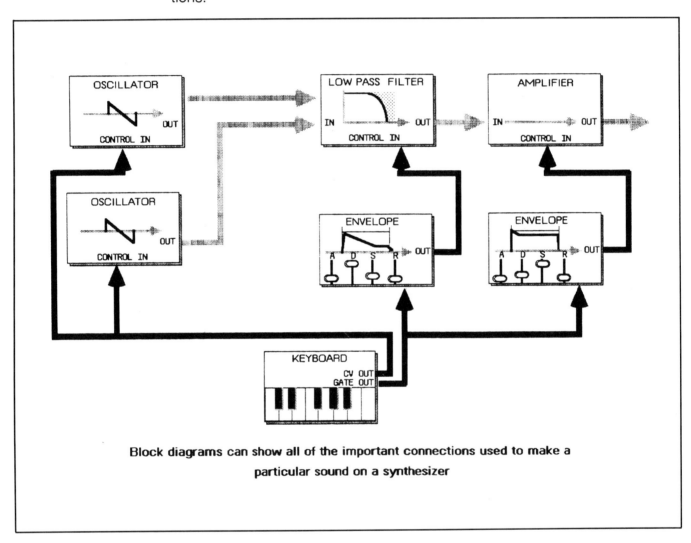

Block diagrams can show all of the important connections used to make a particular sound on a synthesizer

We will use block diagrams to show the interaction between a particular controller and individual sources and modifiers. Once we examine all of the individual control possibilities, block diagrams will be used to show more complex arrangements of multiple functions. This will make it possible to diagram the specific arrangements of sources, modifiers, and controllers necessary to produce specific sounds and effects.

These complete diagrams represent a "recipe" for sounds that can be set up on any synthesizer with similar functions. Many of these diagrams will be presented at the end of this lesson, and in Lessons Four and Five.

The Tool Kit   Every synthesizer has a collection of different controllers. These functions are the basic tools of musical expression. Theoretically, any controller can be used to affect any controllable device. However, for reasons of practicality and performer preferences, certain controllers have become associated with certain types of musical expression. This evolution is reflected by the presence of pitch and mod wheels, dynamic keyboards, foot pedals, breath controllers, and various other specialized controllers on most synthesizers available today.

When learning to play an acoustic instrument, the musician learns by making associations between physical actions and changes in a sound's pitch, timbre, and loudness. Physical skills are reinforced with ear-training (and vice versa). This is not necessarily true of synthesizers. With the exception of manual controllers, the changes that occur in a sound are not directly connected with the physical actions of the player. For this reason, a great deal of basic synthesizer technique is more reliant upon ear training than physical action.

It is vitally important for the synthesist to learn to associate different types of sounds (and changes in the parameters of sound) with the possible control connections between different sources and modifiers (see Lesson Four).

When the basic ear-training skills are mastered, the synthesizer becomes a sound designer's tool kit. It can be "customized" into a variety of distinctly different kinds of musical instruments. Each of these instruments can utilize several eloquent means of musical expression.

Once the instrument is designed, the musician can develop and perfect the physical skills required to perform creatively.

THE TOOL KIT

Master Controllers

A polyphonic synthesizer is one that has several (typically six or eight) identical synthesizers built into it. Each of these internal synthesizers becomes a "voice." The number of voices a synthesizer has will generally determine the number of notes that can be played simultaneously on the instrument.

The **master controller** of a synthesizer is the main area of physical interaction between the performer and the voices within the instrument. It is easy to take this controller for granted because it is such an integral part of an instrument. However, it should be understood there is no direct connection between the physical device and the sounds it articulates.

At the very least, the master controller provides the means for articulation. Many master controllers also provide the means for dynamics and modulation as well.

The most common type is the piano or organ style keyboard. Others include guitar, wind, and drum controllers. We will use the keyboard to examine the basic functions of these controllers as a group. Although they are played in different ways, the master controller of any synthesizer must provide the same basic types of control signals.

When a key is depressed on a synthesizer, at least two different types of control signals are generated. First, a timing signal called a **gate** is generated. The key is like an on/off switch. When a key is down, the gate "turns on" (it stays on as long as the key is down). When a key is up, the gate "turns off." This signal is used to activate a voice within the instrument. When more than one key is held down, one gate is generated for each key depressed (up to the number of voices in the instrument).

The second type of signal generated by the master controller is called **key code (or keyboard CV).** The key code identifies the specific key that is depressed. The signal is most commonly used to control pitch. For polyphonic instruments, a separate key code is generated for each voice when more than one key is held down at a time. It is not usually necessary to show the key code connection between the keyboard and the source oscillators. It can be taken for granted. It is important to show it if it is used to control some other parameter (see examples at the end of this lesson).

Many master controllers can produce manually variable signals that can be used for dynamics and modulation. These are examined below.

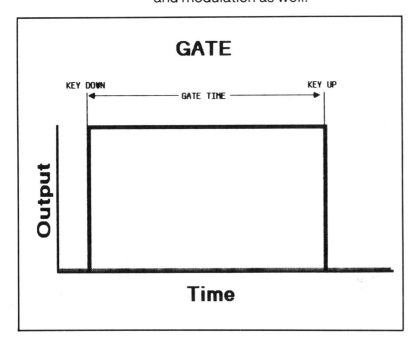

THE TOOL KIT

Envelope Generators

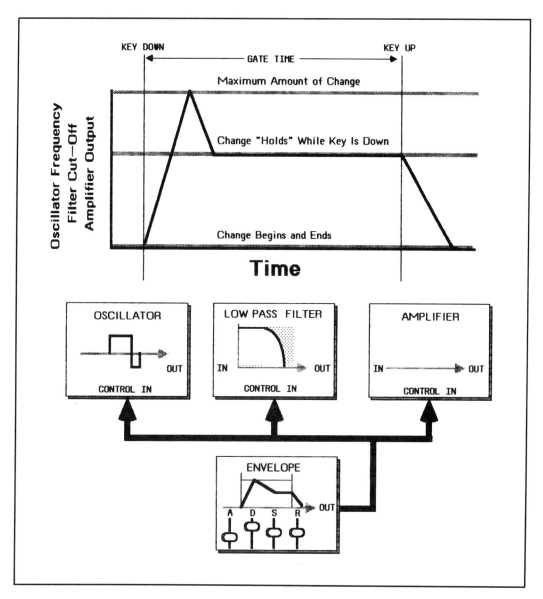

The **envelope generator** (sometimes called **ADSR** or **contour generator**) may be the most important type of controller in a synthesizer. The proper use of this flexible and versatile function is essential to the design of almost any sound. A very thorough demonstration of the envelope generator is given in Lesson Three.

The most common use of an envelope generator is to control overall changes in timbre and/or loudness. For this reason, most synthesizers have at least two dedicated envelope generators, one for the filter and one for the amplifier.

All envelope generators work in the same way. Their output changes between two or more levels. The rate of time between the level changes is variable. The cycle of change is started when a gate signal is sent to the envelope generator from the master controller. This is almost always associated with a key depression; but it can also be initiated by a sequencer, an arpeggiator or an LFO (more about these in Volume Two).

It is not necessary to show this connection between the keyboard gate and the envelope generators in most block diagrams. Like the keyboard CV connection to source oscillators, this can be taken for granted with virtually any keyboard synthesizer. It is, however, important to realize that a signal must be sent to the envelope generator in order to start its cycle of changes.

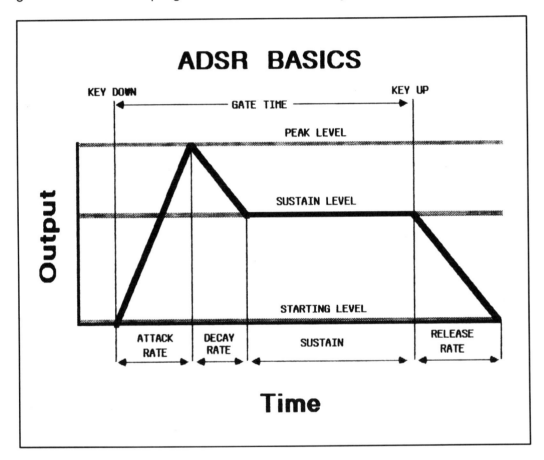

The ADSR is a typical envelope generator. The letters in its name are the initials of its variable parameters: **Attack** rate, **Decay** rate, **Sustain** level, and **Release** rate.

The ADSR's output will change between three levels: starting level, peak level, and sustain level. The order of the change is always the same: peak, sustain, and finally—back to the start again.

THE TOOL KIT

When a key is depressed, the ADSR's output will begin changing from the starting level to the peak level.

Once the peak level is reached, the output will immediately begin changing to the sustain level.

The output will hold at the sustain level as long as a gate is present (a key is down).

When the gate is removed (key is released), the ADSR's level will return to the starting level.

The rate of time between these changes is variable from virtually instantaneous to quite long (several seconds).

At first, it might seem that these are the only four parameters associated with the use of an ADSR. There are, in fact, six parameters to keep track of when using this kind of envelope. Aside from the four previously mentioned ones, there are the two used to set the starting and peak levels. The actual sliders or knobs associated with these two levels will change depending upon what parameter is being controlled. The envelope demonstrations in the video present a very simple and consistent approach for setting these different rates and levels.

The starting level is set manually. There are usually no more than four possibilities for this parameter: oscillator frequency or pulse width, filter cut-off point, or amplifier output level. This setting represents the point from which the change will begin (and end).

The peak level is set with the envelope depth (sometimes called envelope amount, or envelope modulation) control. The setting of this parameter will determine the maximum amount of change caused by the ADSR.

The sustain level is set with ADSR sustain control. This represents the point where the change will "stabilize" if a key is held for a length of time. It can be set anywhere from the starting level up to the peak level.

Attack is the rate of change from the starting to peak levels. It is set with the ADSR's attack control.

Decay is the rate of change from the peak level to the sustain level. This is set with the decay control.

The rate of change from the sustain point back to the starting level is called release. It is set with the, you guessed it, release control.

THE TOOL KIT

Digital technology has made it practical to produce envelope generators with more than three levels and rates. For example, the digital envelope generators on the Yamaha DX7 have four rates and levels; and the Casio CZ 101 has envelopes with eight rates and levels. Although more sophisticated, these digital envelope generators still work in the same manner as the traditional ADSR. The output will cycle between several different variable levels (always in the same order). One of these levels will function as the sustain level. The rate of change between each level is also variable.

Throughout the video and this manual there are numerous examples of the use of envelopes to control synthesizer parameters.

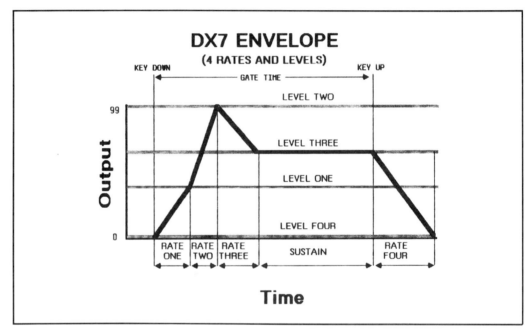

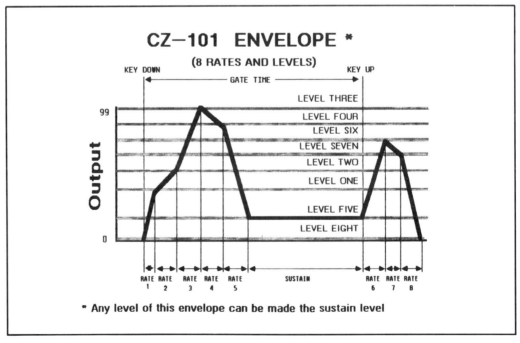

THE TOOL KIT

Low Frequency Oscillator

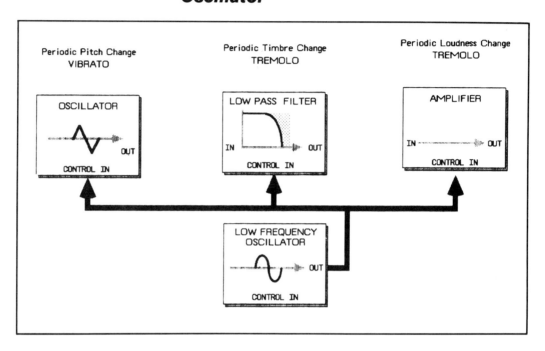

The **low frequency oscillator** is very similar to the audio oscillator. The main difference between the two (as their names imply) is their operating frequencies. Audio oscillators are meant to be sources and therefore, operate in a range of frequencies between 20Hz and 20KHz. Low frequency oscillators are meant to be controllers and operate at rates that are generally below 20Hz. Unlike source oscillators, the frequency of LFOs is not usually controlled by the keyboard.

The typical LFO generates a number of different geometric wave-shapes that can be used to produce repeating changes in a controllable parameter. This type of regular—continuous change—is referred to as **modulation.** The most common types of musical modulation are **vibrato** (a smooth fluctuation in pitch) and **tremolo** (a smooth fluctu-ate in timbre and/or loudness). The LFO demonstration in Lesson Three gives examples of each of these types of modulation.

There are three main variables associated with an LFO. **Rate** will determine the tempo of the repeating change produced by the LFO. **Depth** will determine the overall amount of change. A third variable — **delay,** is often available. Delay controls the LFO's amplitude (depth) over time, allowing the effect to be slowly faded into a sound. This is very useful for vibrato and tremolo effects.

THE TOOL KIT

Sample and Hold

A controller associated with the LFO is the **sample and hold (S/H).** It is a new type of function — a **control processor.** The S/H has both a control input and a waveform input. The control input is connected to an LFO square wave called a **clock.** The clock determines the rate of the S/H output. The waveshape input is typically connected to a noise source. Sometimes the output of this device is simply labeled "Random" and it is shown as an alternative LFO waveshape. Occasionally, the waveform input of the S/H can be connected to several of the LFO waveshapes as well as the noise source.

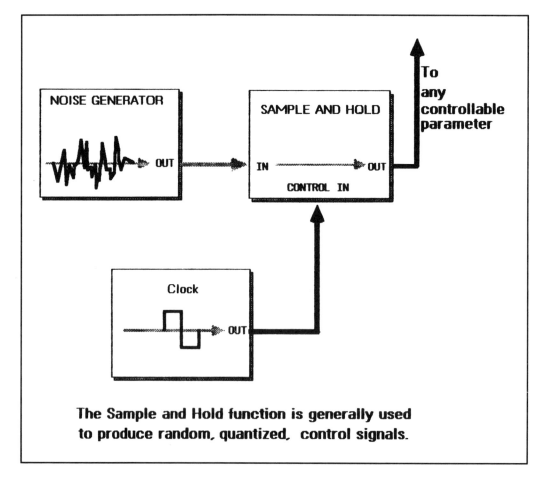

The Sample and Hold function is generally used to produce random, quantized, control signals.

THE TOOL KIT

An S/H works like this: At the beginning of each cycle of the clock, the device "samples" the amplitude of the signal connected to its waveform input. (FIG. 17) This value becomes the output of the S/H until the next cycle of the clock (when a new sample is taken and then "held"). The shape of the input wave and its frequency relative to the clock determine the type of output pattern produced by this device.

A random waveform input, like a noise generator, will produce a random stream of discrete pitches when the S/H is used to control oscillator frequency. A periodic waveshape, like a sawtooth, will produce a repeating pattern of pitches. By changing the rate of either the input LFO or the clock, a myriad of pyramid and staircase glissandos can be produced.

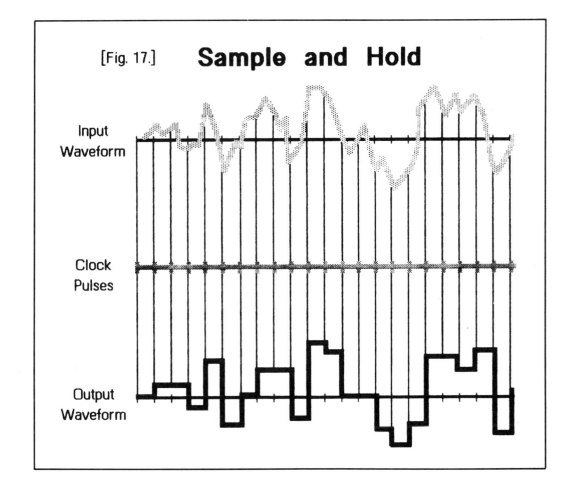

[Fig. 17.] **Sample and Hold**

Input Waveform

Clock Pulses

Output Waveform

THE TOOL KIT

Audio Modulation

The type of timbre produced acoustically by such sources as gongs, cymbals, and bells have non-harmonic partials in their spectrums. The standard geometric waveshapes (sawtooth, pulse, and triangle) available on analog synthesizers have only harmonic partials in their spectrums and are, by themselves, inappropriate for producing this kind of timbre.

Audio modulation is a powerful tool for producing waveshapes with non-harmonic timbres on analog synthesizers. As the term "audio" implies, it is necessary to have an audio frequency (above 20 Hz) oscillator that can be used to control a source oscillator's frequency or amplitude. This controller is referred to as the **modulator.**

On many synthesizers, the LFO can be tuned above 20Hz making it useful as an audio modulator. However, for reasons explained below, it is sometimes useful to have a modulator whose frequency can be controlled from the keyboard. As a result, synthesizers provide a "cross mod" function that allows the output of one source oscillator to be used to control (modulate) the frequency of amplitude of another source oscillator.

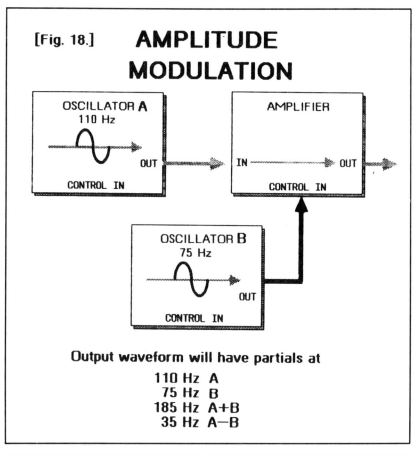

[Fig. 18.] AMPLITUDE MODULATION

Output waveform will have partials at

110 Hz A
75 Hz   B
185 Hz A+B
35 Hz   A−B

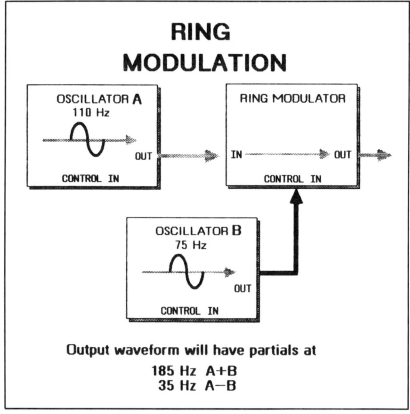

RING MODULATION

Output waveform will have partials at

185 Hz A+B
35 Hz   A−B

Amplitude Modulation (AM)

Amplitude modulation at audio frequencies will generate new partials in the source's spectrum. These new partials are called **sidebands** because their frequencies will be at the sum and difference of the source and controller frequencies (see FIG. 18). A separate pair of sidebands will be generated for each partial in either waveform. The results in an incredibly complex partial structure with many non-harmonic partials (the original two spectrums plus the sums and differences of each of their partials). The resulting sound has a pitched metallic timbre.

Ring Modulation (RM)

A **ring modulator** is a specialized modifier that makes use of a variation of this amplitude modulation technique. The amplitude of a source oscillator is controlled by the amplitude of an audio modulator. The output of a ring modulator will be a waveform with partials at the *sum* and *difference* frequencies of these two oscillators (as well as the sums and differences of each of their partials). The frequencies of the original spectrums will not be present in the output waveform. Unlike normal amplitude modulation spectrums, the ring modulator spectrum will have very few (if any) partials that are harmonically related. The resulting timbres will not give the listener a strong sense of pitch, since there is no fundamental present in the spectrum.

THE TOOL KIT

Frequency Modulation (FM)

Modulating a source oscillator's frequency with an audio modulator will also produce a timbre change. There is a type of synthesis based entirely upon this principle (called **FM synthesis,** of course). This will be examined and demonstrated in detail in Lesson Five. On most analog synthesizers, it is not feasible to use FM as the main technique of timbre production and control. It is, however, a useful timbre modifying tool. Here are the key things to keep in mind about FM on analog synthisizers.

▶ Like AM and ring modulation, FM can be used to produce complex non-harmonic spectrums.

▶ FM produces sidebands at intervals equal to the controlling oscillator's frequency.

▶ The interval tuning between the source and modulator will determine the overall spectrum of the resulting sound.

▶ As the modulation depth is increased, more and more sidebands will be heard.

▶ As more sidebands are introduced into the spectrum, the original frequencies will diminish in amplitude.

These audio modulation techniques can be quite useful to the sound designer. When making gong, bell, and cymbal type timbres, it is often desirable to keep the timbre consistant throughout the keyboard range. This can be done by using the keyboard to control the pitch of both the source and modulator. This occurs because in all of the above audio modulation techniques, the timbre produced is determined by the interval tuning between the source and modulator. Controlling both from the keyboard will keep this interval, and therefore, the timbre, constant.

Audio modulation can also be used to effectively color a sound to produce the rasps and growls associated with many reed and brass instruments. For these effects it is not necessary to control the pitch of the modulator with the keyboard. This is demonstrated in Lesson Four.

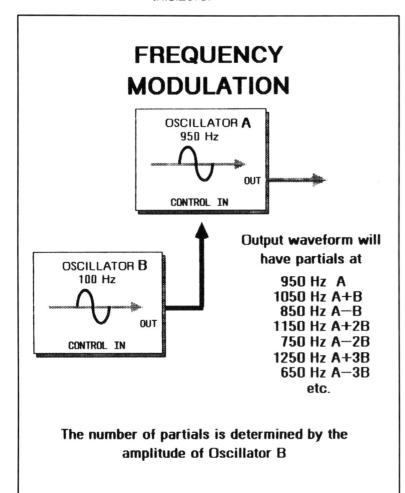

FREQUENCY MODULATION

OSCILLATOR **A**
950 Hz

OUT

CONTROL IN

OSCILLATOR **B**
100 Hz

OUT

CONTROL IN

Output waveform will have partials at

950 Hz A
1050 Hz A+B
850 Hz A−B
1150 Hz A+2B
750 Hz A−2B
1250 Hz A+3B
650 Hz A−3B
etc.

The number of partials is determined by the amplitude of Oscillator B

THE TOOL KIT

Manual Controllers

Manual controllers provide the performer with the means of physical interaction necessary to express musical ideas. The master controller of a synthesizer is the most obvious manual controller. The first synthesizers only had simple organ-type keyboards and no other dedicated manual controllers. Musicians soon discovered ways of manipulating various knobs and sliders on these instruments in order to perform dynamics and modulation as well as basic melodic articulation.

This was the beginning of the evolution of several different types of specialized manual controllers. In general, these devices produce a control signal whose amplitude is directly dependent upon a particular physical action of the player. This continuously variable control signal can be routed to the control input of one or more synthesizer functions, giving the musician direct physical control over various sound parameters.

Velocity

Many keyboards will produce a control signal with an amplitude that is determined by the speed at which keys are depressed. Some instruments will also generate an additional **velocity** signal that is related to the speed that keys are released. This velocity signal is most commonly used to achieve piano-like dynamics by controlling the loudness and/or timbre of each note played on the keyboard.

Some instruments have envelopes with controllable rates. Using velocity to control, attack, and release rates gives each individual note played its own velocity dependent envelope shape.

Controlling pitch with velocity can produce some interesting effects. One technique helpful in emulating certain wind instrument styles is to use velocity to cause an oscillator's pitch to go very slightly sharp or flat with quick attacks. There are several examples on the video of different uses of velocity control.

Pressure

Pressure, sometimes called **after-touch,** is a control signal with an amplitude directly related to the force applied to a key while it is held down. Most often this is used to control modulation depth (to phrase vibrato, tremolo, etc.) and filter cutoff or amplifier level (for crescendos, etc.).

Another useful control connection for pressure is oscillator frequency. This allows the performer to bend and slur notes. It is also a nice alternative to LFO vibrato. The player can manually phrase the vibrato amount and rate so that it is rhythmically in time with the tempo of the piece (just as a violin, guitar, or flute player would). This can be much more musically satisfying, to both the listener and the player, than LFO vibrato. There are several examples of this technique throughout the tape.

THE TOOL KIT

The Bender

Many synthesizers have a specialized device that is used to bend pitch (often it can be used to raise and lower filter cut- off and amplifier level as well). The most common form of this controller is the **wheel,** but there are several variations on this device. Generally, the amount of pitch bend is determined by the physical displacement of the controller (sharp in one direction and flat in another). Often the **bender** is spring loaded. This forces it to return to its starting position when released. The action of a bender is very much like that of a string under tension. Indeed, benders are used all the time to emulate guitar-style pitch bends.

Some instruments allow the player to adjust the maximum amount of change caused by a full swing of the bender. Others offer a selection of two or more intervals. There are many bender examples on the video. The one in Lesson Three shows some alternatives to the standard whole step bend that has become such a synthesizer cliche.

The Mod Controller

A similar device to the bender is the **mod controller.** Like the bender it is often a wheel. The mod controller is not always spring loaded. It is used to control the amount of modulation occurring in a sound, and therefore, it is often desirable to move it to a particular position and be able to leave it there.

Some synthesizers combine both the bender and mod functions into one device that can be displaced in two directions (up and down, left and right). An example of this is shown in Lesson Four.

All of the above controllers give the performer *direct physical access* to sound parameters with his/her hands. There are a variety of controllers that use other physical actions. Among the most popular are foot pedals and breath controllers.

It is important to realize that regardless of the physical action used to initiate the parameter change, all of these devices produce a control signal that has an amplitude which is directly controllable by the performer's actions. The connections between the controller and various synthesizer functions will determine the sound change caused by the device.

The variety and flexibility of these control connections allow the synthesist to develop and perfect distinctive styles of musical expression.

The Secrets

How can these tools be applied to making imitative or innovative sounds? Is it possible to develop a general purpose set of rules and procedures that can be applied to sound design on any synthesizer?

Many synthesists approach making sounds in an intuitive, trial-and-error manner. This is certainly a valid (if not efficient) approach. However, with no standard method to build from, the number of possible choices, connections, and parameter settings can become a formidable (sometimes overwhelming) obstacle to creativity. Too often, the sound designer will settle for a sound that is not quite what he had in mind. It is not necessary to "re-invent the wheel" every time a new sound is made. In fact, except for unusual situations, it should not take more than a minute or so to make a sound from "scratch" on a synthesizer.

There are three "secrets" to making effective sounds. They can be applied to any type of synthesizer — analog or digital. They are based on the physics of music and our subjective perception, not on the particular functions of any one type of synthesizer.

THE SECRETS

The introduction to Lesson One on the tape made the point that a listener's mind will automatically try to associate sounds with imagery. These images are based on past experiences. The basis of the secrets of analog and digital synthesis is the exploitation of this aspect of human perception. Often the synthesist must approach sound design as a magician and impersonator. The sound designer can use sonic slight-of-hand and misdirection to lead listeners to specific conclusions about the created sound. When the proper clues are provided in the proper context, they will be reinforced by subjective experience. The result is an effective sonic illusion.

What are these clues?

1. Basic Timbre: The mind will associate the basic timbre of a sound with a particular acoustic source. (If you can hear it, then it must be coming from somewhere.) Certain overall partial structures are related to different kinds of sources. The source selection on an analog synthesizer and the carrier/modulator ratio (see Lesson Five) on an FM synthesizer will determine a sound's overall spectrum.

2. Tone Production: Changes in timbre over the duration of a note provide the listener with vital clues about what manner of tone production was used to create the sound. Was it plucked, bowed, blown, struck, etc.? This clue is almost always associated with a *timbre envelope.* At first, it might seem that there are an endless number of possible envelope parameter settings. Believe it or not, there are only two basic envelopes that can be used for most sounds. The timbre envelope is usually the filter envelope on analog instruments and the modulator envelope on FM instruments.

3. Style Emulation: This is probably the most important, and least utilized clue. Performance technique, perhaps more than any other clue, is the strongest indicator of what kind of instrument is producing a sound. (Simply bending a note a whole step sharp will convince most people they are hearing a "guitar" regardless of the overall spectrum and timbre envelope.) The various manual controllers available on a synthesizer offer the player many options for different kinds of stylistic performances.

These clues can be used to imitate instrument sounds, such as brass, strings, woodwinds, etc., or to create new sounds depending on how they are put together.

THE SECRETS

1. Basic Timbre

It is possible to classify virtually any musical instrument (or any sound producing mechanism) into one of four categories of overall spectrum. This chart (FIG. 19) lists the different instruments and synthesizer sources associated with these four overall spectrums.

A good way to start when designing a sound, is to select a source (or sources) with the appropriate overall timbre. On many instruments, this is simple a choice between sawtooth and pulse waves.

[Fig. 19.]

Comparison of Acoustic & Synthesizer Sources

OVERALL SPECTRUM	ACOUSTIC SOURCE	ANALOG SOURCE	FM SOURCE	INSTRUMENT TIMBRE
ALL HARMONIC PARTIALS	Open Air Columns Vibrating Strings	Sawtooth Narrow Pulse	Modulator Ratio 1	Brass, Strings Guitar, Bass Woodwinds
ODD HARMONIC PARTIALS	Closed Air Column	Square Triangle	Modulator Ratio 2	Clarinet Recorder Whistles, Organ
NON HARMONIC PARTIALS	Membranes Suspended Bars	Audio Mod (AM - FM) Source Mixing	Additive Sine waves Modulator Ratio Non Integer	Electric Piano Bells, Vibes Cymbals, Tympani Tom-Toms
"RANDOM" HARMONIC PARTIALS	Transients Rushing Air Snares	Noise Generator	Modulator with Feedback	Breath, Drums Wind, Thunder Mechanical Action

There are two general methods of producing sounds used on musical instruments. We know now that in any acoustic instrument a mass must be made to vibrate in order to produce sound. The method of excitation greatly effects the development of the sound's overall timbre and loudness changes.

Any of the instruments in a symphonic orchestra could be placed into one or two groups based on its manner of tone production. One group would contain only instruments that required **continuous excitation** to produce a sound. The other would contain only those instruments that required **momentary excitation** to produce a sound.

Continuous Excitation Instruments	Momentary Excitation Instruments
BRASS **WOODWINDS** **BOWED STRINGS** **VOICES** **WHISTLES** **ORGANS*** *Electronic organs have an instantaneous attack. Pipe organs have a slight attack at the start of a note.	**PLUCKED STRINGS** **PIANOS** **PITCHED PERCUSSION** **UNPITCHED PERCUSSION**

Continuous Excitation

Any instrument that needs a constant application of force (like breath, bowing, etc.), requires continuous excitation to produce a sound. The sound will continue as long as the force is applied.

We can make some very general assumptions about the loudness and timbre envelopes of such sounds:

All instruments that require continuous excitation will have some degree of **slow attack.** They will also be capable of holding a note's loudness steady for long periods of musical time (sustain). When the excitation stops, the sound will not stop instantly, instead it will take a certain amount of time to fade away (release). For example, in a wind instrument like a trumpet, even if a player "chokes off" a note, the sound will not stop instantly. It takes a small (but noticeable) amount of time for the air to stop vibrating in the horn.

The timbre envelope will have the same basic shape as the loudness envelope. In general, the timbre of a continuous excitation instrument will change in the following manner:

THE SECRETS

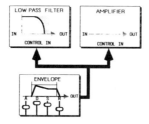

At the beginning of a note, the sound's spectrum will be quite simple (often containing just the fundamental). During the attack portion of the sound, the partials in the overall spectrum will "build up" over the fundamental until a maximum brightness in the tone is reached. This peak is often brighter than the timbre of a held tone (Such is the case when a player "over blows" a note).

The timbre will change again during the release of a note. Partials will fade out of the spectrum in the opposite order in which they appeared.

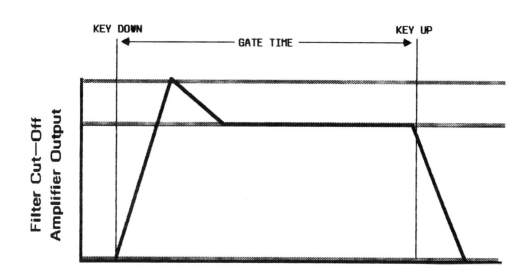

The RATE settings of a continuous excitation envelope are determined
by the rhythmic activity of the melody. Rapid passages will have quicker
rates.
The SUSTAIN LEVEL can be set to maximum for sounds like organs and legato strings.
Levels in between minimum and maximum are effective for wind instruments.

THE SECRETS

Momentary Excitation

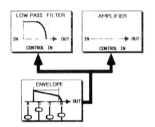

Instruments that are plucked or struck require only momentary excitation to produce sound. As with continuous excitation instruments, it is possible to make some generalizations about this type of sound's loudness and timbre envelopes.

The attack of such an instrument is virtually **instantaneous.** It is at its loudest and brightest at the instant of the attack. This type of instrument is not capable of "holding" a sound for long periods of time. Its loudness envelope will have no sustain.

As the sound fades away, its timbre will become continuously less bright. The partials in its spectrum will fade out in a descending order.

———————————

These two basic timbre envelopes are demonstrated in Lesson Three. Virtually every musical example on the video tape uses one or the other of these two basic envelope shapes.

The specific settings of rates and levels are, of course, very significant to the final results. Rates are generally determined by the rhythmic requirements of a part. Levels, more often than not, are a matter of personal preference.

It is very easy to simulate either of these two envelopes on any synthesizer with an ADSR, or any of the more sophisticated digital envelope generators. The loudness changes are accomplished by using the envelope to control the amplifier, and timbre changes by controlling filter cut-off (carrier and modulator levels on an FM synth).

We are not saying that all sounds exhibit these exact loudness and timbre envelope characteristics. In terms of our perception, however, these general timbre and loudness changes can simulate (in a broad sense) the type of tone production of virtually any instrument.

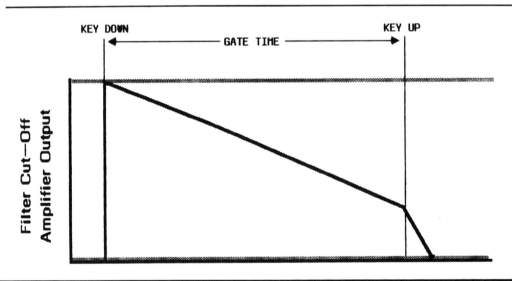

The ATTACK RATE of a momentary excitation envelope will always be instantaneous. The DECAY and RELEASE RATES will determine how "percussive" a sound is. The ones shown here simulate a piano. A note will ring for some time while a key is held down, then stop quickly when it is let up.

Momentary excitation envelopes have minimal (if any) SUSTAIN LEVELS.

THE SECRETS

3. Style Emulation

Selecting the proper overall spectrum and setting up the right timbre and loudness envelopes are very important to our general perception of a sound. However, **articulation**, **phrasing,** and **subtlety of expression** are really the main clues to the origin of an imitative or innovative sound. The importance of developing and perfecting various performance techniques cannot be emphasized enough.

Music theory and instrumental performance are not the subjects of this course, but the sound designer/musician must be just as aware of musical considerations, as of sound parameters. Throughout this tape, and in Lessons Eight and Ten of the next volume in this series, there are numerous examples of different stylistic approaches to performance.

It is as important to imitate the style of a player and the performance "quirks" of an instrument, as it is to imitate the sound itself. This does not mean that synthesists are limited to imitation alone. The synthesizer is, by definition, a general purpose music machine. In a sense, it has no characteristic sound of its own. By imitating various aspects of other instruments, the synthesist can put creative ideas into any musical context desired. Imitation serves as a "jump off point" for any sound you want to make.

The Sound Designer's Cook Book

Here is a collection of block diagrams of various synthesizer "patches." All of the sounds made in Lesson Three are included here as well as diagrams for many other types of sounds and effects.

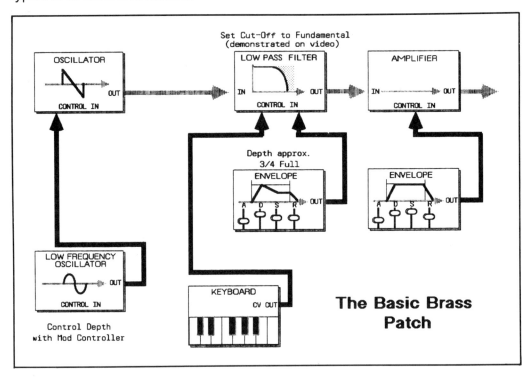

The Basic Brass Patch

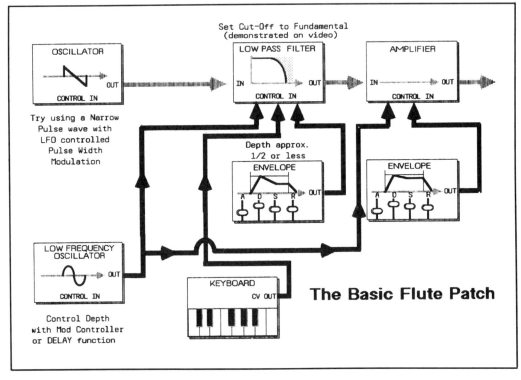

The Basic Flute Patch

**THE
SOUND DESIGNER'S
COOK BOOK**

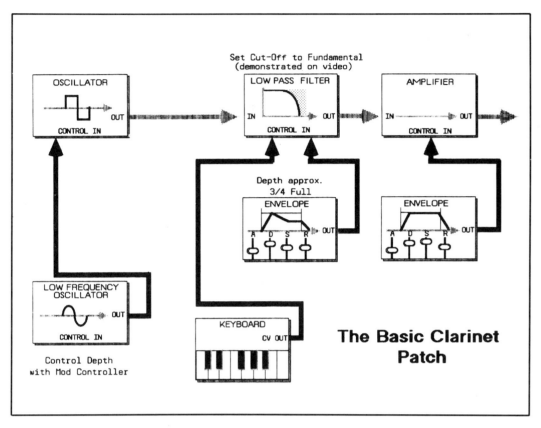

Set Cut-Off to Fundamental
(demonstrated on video)

Depth approx.
3/4 Full

**The Basic Clarinet
Patch**

Control Depth
with Mod Controller

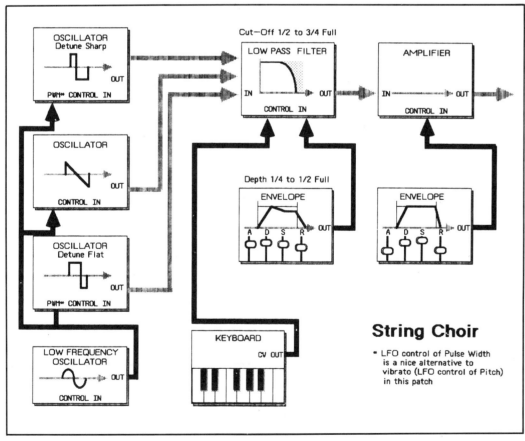

Cut—Off 1/2 to 3/4 Full

Depth 1/4 to 1/2 Full

String Choir

* LFO control of Pulse Width
is a nice alternative to
vibrato (LFO control of Pitch)
in this patch

73

THE
SOUND DESIGNER'S
COOK BOOK

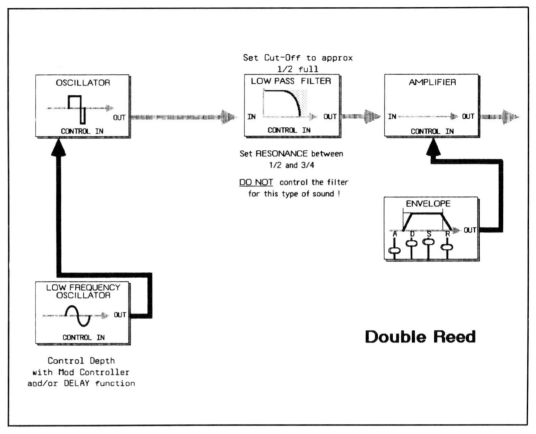

Set Cut-Off to approx
1/2 full

Set RESONANCE between
1/2 and 3/4

DO NOT control the filter
for this type of sound !

Double Reed

Control Depth
with Mod Controller
and/or DELAY function

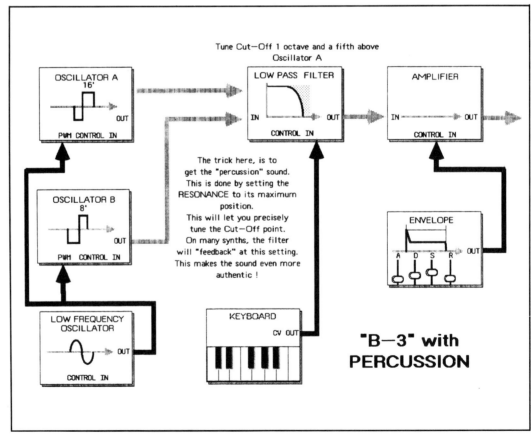

Tune Cut-Off 1 octave and a fifth above
Oscillator A

The trick here, is to
get the "percussion" sound.
This is done by setting the
RESONANCE to its maximum
position.
This will let you precisely
tune the Cut-Off point.
On many synths, the filter
will "feedback" at this setting.
This makes the sound even more
authentic !

**"B—3" with
PERCUSSION**

**THE
SOUND DESIGNER'S
COOK BOOK**

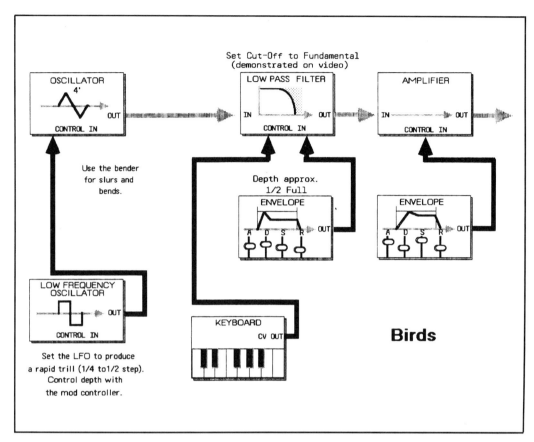

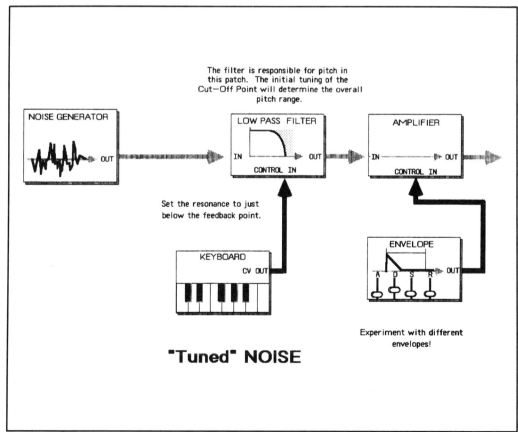

**THE
SOUND DESIGNER'S
COOK BOOK**

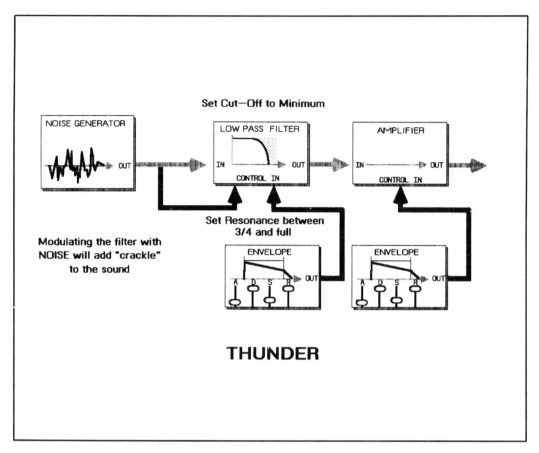

Set Cut—Off to Minimum

NOISE GENERATOR

LOW PASS FILTER

AMPLIFIER

Set Resonance between 3/4 and full

Modulating the filter with NOISE will add "crackle" to the sound

ENVELOPE

ENVELOPE

THUNDER

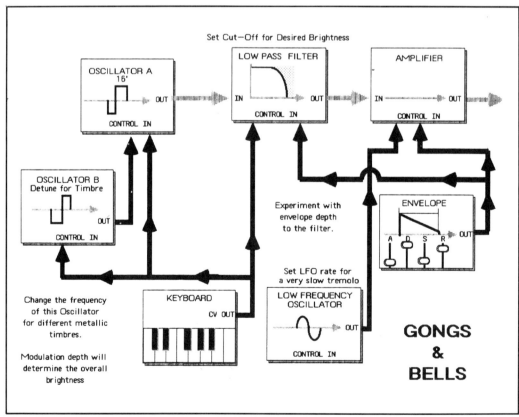

Set Cut—Off for Desired Brightness

OSCILLATOR A
16'

LOW PASS FILTER

AMPLIFIER

OSCILLATOR B
Detune for Timbre

Experiment with envelope depth to the filter.

ENVELOPE

Change the frequency of this Oscillator for different metallic timbres.

Modulation depth will determine the overall brightness

Set LFO rate for a very slow tremolo

KEYBOARD

LOW FREQUENCY OSCILLATOR

**GONGS
&
BELLS**

**THE
SOUND DESIGNER'S
COOK BOOK**

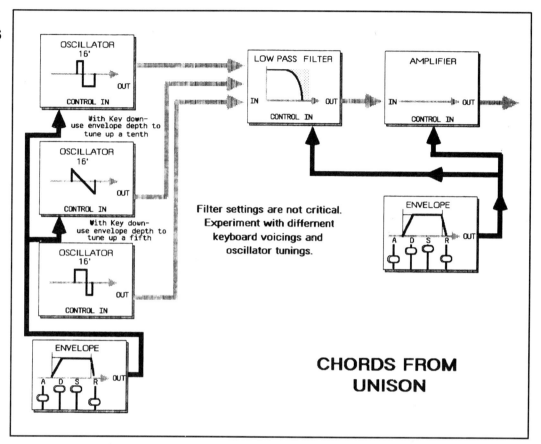

With Key down-
use envelope depth to
tune up a tenth

With Key down-
use envelope depth to
tune up a fifth

Filter settings are not critical.
Experiment with differnent
keyboard voicings and
oscillator tunings.

**CHORDS FROM
UNISON**

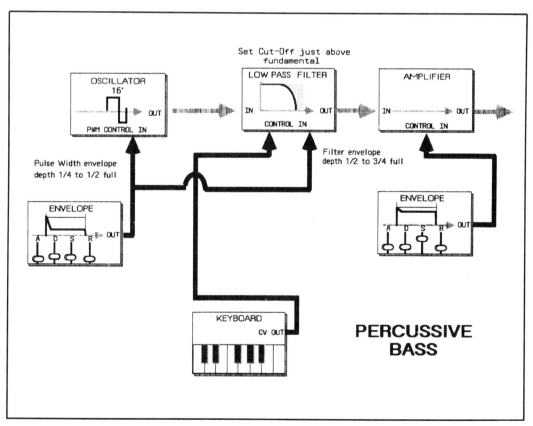

Set Cut-Off just above
fundamental

Pulse Width envelope
depth 1/4 to 1/2 full

Filter envelope
depth 1/2 to 3/4 full

**PERCUSSIVE
BASS**

NOTES:

LESSON FOUR:
Synthesizers & Editing Techniques

Special Synthesizer Features

As we promised in this lesson on the tape, "It's time for a change of pace . . . " In this section are a series of diagrams and notes that relate to the special features demonstrated in the beginning of Lesson Four.

There are 46 mini-demonstrations that show a variety of different synthesizer features. These demonstrations are not meant to be a comprehensive representation of any particular instrument (or instruments). That would be beyond the scope of this series. However, this is a sampling of the overall variety of features found on synthesizers in general. As you watch and listen to these examples, you can follow along in the manual to learn more about the function(s) being shown.

We demonstrate several features on each instrument, then move on to the next one. Sometimes the same feature is demonstrated on more than one instrument. The information below is presented in the order that the features are introduced.

Stereo Chorus

A **chorus** function is a type of modifier. It works on the same principle as the ensemble effect created by detuning oscillators (See Lesson Two). Here's how it works. The output of the synthesizer's amplifier is electronically duplicated and delayed in time by a small amount (several milliseconds). This is equivalent to detuning two identical sources, except a chorus function "detunes" the audio output of the synthesizer itself. When the original and delayed signals are combined, a beating effect is heard. The delay amount is varied with an LFO sine wave varying the beating rate. This adds a very "lush" quality to timbres, and simulates the effect of several sources all playing together (like a string choir). The **stereo chorus** demonstrated on the tape routes different variations of the effect to each side of a stereo mix. This makes the chorus effect even more "spacious."

Sub-Oscillator

The **sub-oscillator** is an additional oscillator output with a frequency of one-half of the oscillator's true tuning. This means it is one octave lower in pitch (see Lesson One). Typically, the waveshape of a sub-oscillator is a square wave. In this demonstration, it is used to simulate the 16' stop of a draw bar organ.

Multi-Function Bender

The bender of the Juno 106 is an example of a manual controller that can alter several different parameters at once. In this demonstration, side to side movement of the bender changes both oscillator frequency and filter cut-off. The amount of change caused by moving the bender to the extreme ends of its range is separately adjustable for both the filter and the oscillator. Pushing the bender towards the back of the instrument alters the amount of LFO modulation controlling the oscillator's pitch (vibrato).

**SPECIAL
SYNTHESIZER
FEATURES**

Left Hand Mute Function

This can be quite useful when playing left hand chords and right hand melody on the same keyboard. The **left hand mute** lowers the loudness of the sound on the left side of the keyboard. This makes it possible to play chords that don't overpower the melody.

Inverted Envelope

The output of an **inverted envelope** is exactly the opposite of the normal envelope (FIG. 20). For example, the release of a normal ADSR is always a change from a higher level to a lower level. When connected to an amplifier, a slow release time will cause the sound to get softer and softer. The same envelope connected to a filter will slowly lower the cut-off point, making the sound duller and duller. The inverted version of the same envelope will cause the opposite of these two effects. As the inverted envelope releases, the sound would get louder or brighter (depending on whether it controlled the filter or the amplifier).

In the JX 3P demo, the same ADSR is used to control both amplifier and the filter. However, the filter envelope is inverted. This causes the sound to get brighter and softer at the same time. The Polaris demonstration is essentially the same. This time, two different envelopes are used, and again, the filter envelope is inverted.

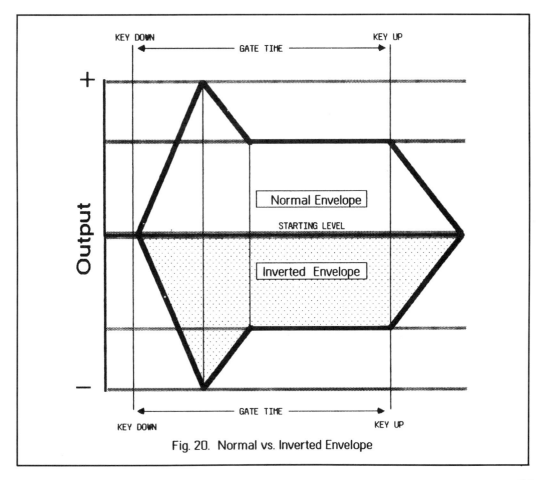

Fig. 20. Normal vs. Inverted Envelope

**SPECIAL
SYNTHESIZER
FEATURES**

LFO with Delay and Random Functions

The JX 3P demonstration shows how the LFO delay function is used to slowly increase the amount (depth) of filter modulation. In this case, the LFO waveshape is random. It is controlling the cut-off point of a resonant filter. This produces a rapidly changing emphasis of random partials in the sound's spectrum. The rate is determined with the LFO rate setting. Delayed LFO amount is also demonstrated with the Juno 106, OB-8, Polaris, EX-800, and CZ-101.

Multi-Timbral Six Track Sequencer

Sequencers will be explored in detail in Volume II of this series, but here is a basic definition. A **sequencer** is a function that can "remember" and repeat a performance. Some sequencers are similar to multi-track recorders. They can record several "over-dubs." The sequencer in the Six-Trak can over-dub up to six monophonic (one note at a time) performances. Each of these six "tracks" can have a different preset sound assigned to it. As you can hear in the demo, there are several different "instruments" playing at once.

Voice Stacking

Stacking means to play several of the voices in an instrument from a single key simultaneously. The Six-Trak allows each of the six voices in a stack to be a different preset sound. By tuning each of the presets used to different pitches, a six note chord (with a different sound for each voice) can be played from a single key.

In the Polaris stacking example, two presets are stacked (or layered). Two voices are played from a single key. Since each voice has two oscillators, four pitches can be played from one key. The keyboard was used to set the pitch intervals between the four oscillators (2 per voice) to create a four note voicing per note.

SPECIAL SYNTHESIZER FEATURES

Multi Mode Arpeggiator

An **arpeggiator**, as its name implies, will arpeggiate the notes of a chord that is played on the keyboard. The rate of the arpeggiation is controlled with an LFO.

The Six-Trak's arpeggiator has two modes: up/down and assign. In the up/down mode, the arpeggiator plays the chord tones in alternating ascending and descending order. In the assign mode, the notes are played repetively in the order in which they are depressed.

The OB-8's arpeggiator has several modes also. The notes can be played in ascending and/or descending order and in a random order as well. Another feature demonstrated with the OB-8 is the transpose function. The arpeggiation can be automatically transposed to different keys (up to five).

Separate ADSR for Pitch Control

The Six-Trak has a separate ADSR to control oscillator frequency independent of filter and amplifier changes. In this sound, the pitch envelope is used to simulate the drop in pitch that occurs during the decay of a tom-tom.

Stereo Split Keyboards

There are several demonstrations that show the use of **split keyboards** on the T-8 and OB-8 synthesizers. On both instruments, it is possible to assign different presets to either side of the keyboard. The boundary between the two sides (called the **split point**) is selectable. The obvious advantage of this feature is that two completely different sounds can be played independently by one player on one instrument. A related function is **layering.** Layering allows two different presets to be played simultaneously from a single key.

The T-8 is a stereo instrument in either the split or layered mode, each preset is routed to one side of a stereo mix. The OB-8 is also a stereo instrument. Each of its eight voices has an independent **pan-pot.** This makes it possibe to ''place'' the voices in various positions within the stereo field.

**SPECIAL
SYNTHESIZER
FEATURES**

8 Voice Pressure and Velocity Sensitivity

The T-8 has a dynamic keyboard. It is both **pressure** and **velocity** sensitive. These dynamics can be used to control various parameters such as modulation depth, filter cut-off, amplifier level, envelope rates, and oscillator frequency. The manner in which each key is played can dramatically effect a sound.

The first demonstration shows how pressure can be used to directly control pitch, timbre, and loudness. Each key takes on an independent tonal character.

The second demo shows a more basic approach to traditional keyboard dynamics. Velocity is controlling both filter cut-off and amplifier level. Pressure is controlling oscillator frequency. Notice the musical control this gives a performer over changes in the "Big Three."

Portamento Bend

This feature allows the sound designer to pre-select an interval of pitch change that will occur at the beginning of each note. The pitch change can be either sharp or flat. The interval can be considerable, like the one used here; or it can be very slight.

This can be helpful in simulating certain types of pitch articulations commonly used on wind and string instruments.

Foot Pedal Controlled Release

This feature of the OB-8 allows a **footswitch** to be used to select between two release settings of the amplifier envelope. The specific set-tings are variable. The release rates used here simulate a piano sustain pedal. A short release occurs with the pedal up, and a long release occurs when the pedal is held down.

LFO Rate Envelope

The OB-8 has a separate envelope to control **LFO rate.** It is similar to an LFO delay control; except instead of modulation depth, it controls modulation rate.

Three Oscillators per Voice

The Memory Moog has three audio oscillators for each voice. The first example (and several others throughout the tape) uses three sources slightly detuned to produce a chorus effect.

In the second example, each oscillator is tuned to a different pitch of a triad. Each key played will sound a three note chord.

ADSR Control of Sync Oscillator

This is an alternative to using a filter for an envelope controlled timbre change. This technique (the sound tool) is fully explained later in this lesson.

Ring Modulator

The **ring modulator** is a modifier that produces timbres with non-harmonic partials in their spectrums *(See Lesson One)*. It is useful in making metallic and bell-like sounds.

**SPECIAL
SYNTHESIZER
FEATURES**

Expanders

An **expander** is a synthesizer that can be remotely controlled from another instrument's master controller. It may or may not have a master controller of its own. The advent of **MIDI** has made it possible (and simple) to do this. In Volume II, this Musical Instrument Digital Interface (MIDI) will be explored and explained.

The Oberheim Expander

The Xpander is a new generation of analog synthesizer. It has many features and controls not found on other synthesizers. The Xpander has six voices, each of which can be programmed independently. The Xpander has a very sophisticated programming matrix. Any of its controllers can be connected to any controllable parameter. It can also assign control signals from external devices (benders, pedals, etc.) to any controllable parameter as well.

The Xpander is designed to be used in conjunction with other instruments (explaining the lack of a keyboard). It can be controlled with keyboard CV, computer, or MIDI signals. In these demonstrations, it was controlled from the keyboard of a Yamaha DX7. The DX7 is used only as a MIDI master controller. It is not making sounds in any of the Xpander demos.

Assignable Velocity and Pressure

The velocity and pressure controls of the master controller can be **assigned** to any controllable parameter on the Xpander. In this demonstration, velocity is used to control the filter and amplifier; and pressure controls modulation depth.

Assignable MIDI Controllers

Any MIDI controller (bender, mod wheel, pedal, breath controller, etc.) can be **assigned** to any controllable parameter. In this case, a MIDI footswitch is used to control release time to simulate a piano pedal.

Multi-Mode Filter

The Xpander has several different filter modes *(see Lesson Two)*. The first sound demonstrated uses a combination **low pass and phase filter.** The second sound uses a resonant **high pass filter.**

Korg EX 800

The Korg EX 800 is a six voice MIDI expander. It has a **stereo chorus, digital envelope, generators,** and a built-in **sequencer** among its many functions.

Output in Four Octaves Simultaneously

The oscillators in the EX 800 can produce outputs in four octaves at once. This is the equivalent to 16', 8', 4', and 2' organ pipes.

Synth Arts

Separate Envelope for Noise Generator

The EX 800 is used to demonstrate how a slight amount of noise mixed into the attack portion of a sound can simulate the scratch of a bow or the breath of a wind player. The *independent* noise envelope makes it possible to remove the noise from the sound after a short period of time. The effect sounds different at both ends of the keyboard because the filter's cut-off point is not controlled from the keyboard. Lower notes have a brighter timbre and sound "scratchy." Higher notes have a duller timbre and sound "breathy."

The Casio CZ-101

The CZ-101 is a digital synthesizer. It has no fiters, and yet, it produces timbres that sound very much like those associated with analog synthesizers. The principle of timbre generation used by this synthesizer is called **phase distortion.** Phase distortion changes a wave's partial structure by literally altering the shape of the wave itself. This is done digitally, by manipulating numerical data. The end result is very similar to the changes in shape caused by modifying an analog waveform with a low pass filter.

The CZ-101 has eight selectable complex waveshapes available from its digital oscillators. An envelope is used to change the waveshape from a sine wave to the selected complex shape. For all practical purposes, you can think of the CZ-101 as having a "digital filter."

Don't be misled by the size of this instrument. It is a very powerful and flexible synthesizer. It has two identical independent audio paths. Each of its eight voices has the digital equivalence of an oscillator, filter, and amplifier. Each of these functions has an independent 8-level envelope generator. Timbre and loudness changes can be scaled by the keyboard. The instrument also has a very complete MIDI implementation (*see Volume II*).

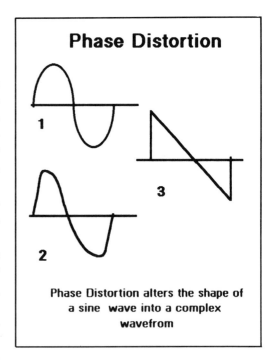

Phase Distortion

1

2

3

Phase Distortion alters the shape of a sine wave into a complex wavefrom

**SPECIAL
SYNTHESIZER
FEATURES**

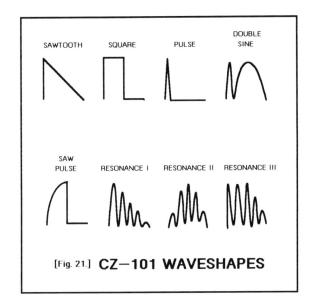

[Fig. 21.] **CZ—101 WAVESHAPES**

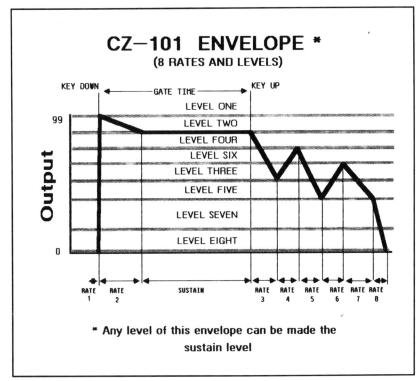

* Any level of this envelope can be made the sustain level

Digital Oscillators

The digital oscillators in the CZ-101 have eight selectable wave-shapes. Besides the typical sawtooth, square, pulse and sine waves, the Casio has several unique waveshapes as well (FIG. 21).

Digital "Filter"

As explained above, there are no filters in this instrument. However, the sound in this demonstration shows how similar this instrument can sound to an analog instrument.

8 Level Digital Envelope Generators

The envelope generators in the CZ-101 are very sophisticated. Each has eight programmable levels and rates. Any one of the levels can be selected as sustain. In this demonstration, the envelopes are programmed to simulate reverb. There is absolutely no reverberation added electronically to the sound. The envelopes are used to provide a very subtle, multi-level release. The resulting loudness changes sound like a high quality reverb unit.

MIDI Expander Capabilities

The CZ-101 can be controlled from any MIDI master controller (in this case, the DX7). The instrument supports MIDI functions.

Editing Techniques

The typical synthesizer has the ability to store many different sounds within its internal memories. Editing is the process of changing these preset sounds in order to make them more appropriate for a particular musical situation. There is certainly nothing wrong with using preset sounds. In fact, many players use nothing but presets. However, if you only use presets, you will be limited to whatever is in the synthesizer's memory and unable to take advantage of the versatility and flexability offered by these remarkable instruments.

You have to know your way around on a synthesizer before you can begin altering sounds. Here are some basic questions that must be answered in order to familiarize yourself with an instrument:

▶What's in the **audio path?** What are the instrument's **sources** and **modifiers?** (See Lesson Two)

▶How are **pitch, timbre,** and **loudness** controlled? What kinds of controllers are available, and where can they be routed?
(See Lesson Three)

Ear Training

Once you've learned your way around on a particular instrument, you can begin to make or alter sounds. Aside from performance, the most exciting thing about working with synthesizers is making sounds that fit particular musical requirements. You can create your own "on call" orchestra of real and imaginary instruments.

There is no big mystery involved in sound creation. If you hear the difference between a sawtooth and a square wave, then you probably have what it takes to be a good sound designer. This is so because sound design, like so many other aspects of music, is just ear-training applied to specific knowledge. If you want to learn a new song by taking it off a record, you can do it by listening for subtle variations of pitch, harmony, and rhythm and applying them to what you know about music theory. Sound design is approached in a similar manner. Start listening to the sounds that constantly occur all around you. Listen for subtle variations in pitch, timbre, and loudness; and apply them to what you know about sound and synthesis. Think about sounds in terms of the "Big Three" and synthesizer functions. How would you go about recreating them on a synthesizer?

> If you own a synthesizer, go through the presets until you find one that you don't completely understand. Try to figure it out. What waveform(s) is(are) being used? Is there any pitch modulation going on? How is the timbre changing? What about the loudness? What kind of envelopes are being used, and what parameters are being controlled? How much of the sound can you block diagram?

What you can't deduce with your ears alone, you can learn from the instrument itself. Carefully alter the parameters in question, one at a time. Listen to the changes that are caused by these explorations. When that sound has revealed its secrets, go on to the next one. Your goal is to be able to tell exactly what is going on in a sound as you hear it. Does that seem difficult? It's really not. It's certainly no more difficult than being

EDITING TECHNIQUES

able to hear the chord changes of a tune by listening to a record. It's a lot less difficult than hearing the exact voicings that are being used in the horn section, or the exact pitches and rhythms being played in the guitar solo. You can do it. Like so many other musical skills, all it requires is patience and practice.

Filling in the Blanks

Many synthesists think of sound design in two different ways: making sounds from scratch, and editing presets. Making a sound from scratch means starting with a "clean slate" and building up a sound from there. (A scratch sound is simply a preset with no unknown parameter settings.) This makes it easy to keep track of alterations and changes as they are made. Editing involves making alterations to a pre-existing sound.

If you stop to think about it, both methods are the same. In either case a preset sound is being edited. A scratch sound is just a preset with no surprises in it. Making a sound from scratch just means that you always start with the same preset. This is like being able to drive to any place in the United States as long as you always start your trip from your mother's driveway.

As your ear-training abilities improve, any preset becomes a scratch sound because it has no unknowns in it. When you want to edit a sound, you can take a kind of "fill in the blanks" approach:

	??	Bass	Oboe	Gong	Thunder
Pitched Sound?	—	YES	YES	YES	NO
Pitch Range?	—	16'	8'	16'	—
Basic Timbre?	—	ALL HARMONICS SAW or PULSE	ALL HARMONICS PULSE	NON-HARMONICS AUDIO MODULATION	RANDOM PARTIALS NOISE GENERATOR
Tone Production?	—	MOMENTARY	CONTINUOUS	MOMENTARY	MOMENTARY
Dynamics?	—	PITCH BEND	PRESSURE MOD DEPTH	VELOCITY LOUDNESS	VELOCITY TIMBRE

EDITING TECHNIQUES

It should not take long to get in the ball park. Then it becomes a matter of finishing touches: Getting the *rates* of the envelopes just right — *Detuning oscillators* to make the sound "fatter" — Setting just the right *LFO rate* and *delay* — Working up the proper *bender technique* — and so on. These final details can make the difference between a *good sound* and a *great one.* They are mostly a matter of taste and experience. The best way to learn what works is by exploring and listening.

Below are block diagrams showing the edits made to the "brass" sound in Lesson Four. In the first example, the sound was altered slightly (by adding audio modulation) to change its character. The sound is changed into something completely different in the second example.

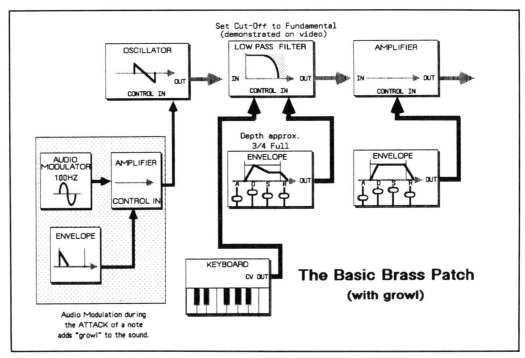

The Basic Brass Patch (with growl)

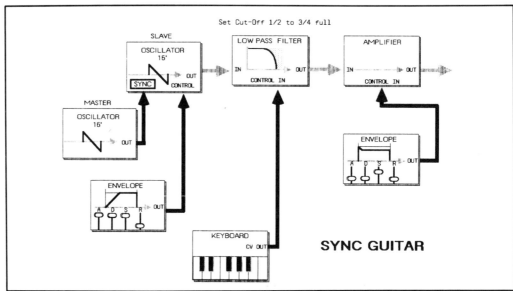

SYNC GUITAR

LESSON FIVE:
FM Synthesis

Frequency Modulation

In Lesson Three, the basic principles of FM were introduced and shown to be an effective way of producing certain types of timbres. The advent of digital technology has made it possible to develop instruments that utilize these principles as the main means of timbre production. At first glance, FM seems very different than subtractive synthesis (synthesis based on the use of filters), because there are different functions and new terminology to learn.

However, we know now that all synthesizers must have certain general functions in common. A synthesizer must allow the musician to control changes in the "Big Three." In this respect, FM instruments are no different from instruments that use filters. They can be very different, however, in the type of timbres that they can produce and the manner in which these timbres change over the course of a note.

FM synthesis provides the sound designer with many new sources of basic waveshapes as well as some very eloquent timbre envelope possibilities. There are only two manufacturers currently making FM instruments (Yamaha and New England Digital). We will take a close look at the most widely available instrument at this time.

The Yamaha DX7

Lesson Five on the tape contains very in-depth demonstrations of the principles and techniques used in FM synthesis. Since a Yamaha DX7 is used for these demonstrations, Lesson Five is also a thorough demonstration of this popular instrument.

Before we can begin an exploration of FM, we have to take a close look at the functions available of the DX7. This is a new generation of synthesizer; and therefore, it has many functions and parameters that don't exist on other instruments. Since it is not an analog instrument, it has no filters. On further examination, we see it has no functions labeled "oscillators" or "amplifiers" as well. The audio path of the DX7 is not fixed. In fact, there are 32 different variations of the audio path. These are called "algorithms" by Yamaha. **Algorithms** will be explained later in this lesson.

Operators

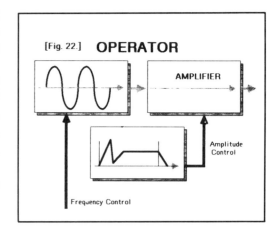

[Fig. 22.] **OPERATOR**

The basic DX7 function is called an **operator.** An operator is actually a multi-function unit. Within each operator, there is the digital equivalent to a sine wave oscillator, an amplifier, and an envelope generator (FIG. 22). The envelope generator controls the output level of the amplifier, and therefore, the sine wave's amplitude. The sine wave's frequency can be manually tuned and can also be controlled by various controllers on the DX7 (such as the keyboard, LFO, bender, etc.).

FREQUENCY MODULATION

An operator, then, is a function that generates a sine wave with controllable frequency and amplitude. All of the synthesis techniques that can be applied to the DX7 are based on only these two types of parameter changes: operator frequency and operator amplitude.

There are six operators per voice in this sixteen-voice instrument.

> **NOTE:** In this series, we use the term "voice" to define one independent sound module within a synthesizer. The number of voices determines the number of notes that can be played simultaneously. Yamaha uses this term to mean also a "pre-programmed sound" or preset. The DX7 can store 32 of these preset "voices" internally. More preset "voices" can be accessed with memory cartridges. For consistency's sake, we will continue to use "voice" as a unit of polyphony, and "preset" as a pre-programmed sound.

Block Diagramming

Block diagrams for this FM instrument are drawn in a different manner to reflect the different mode of synthesis. Each operator is represented by one block. The blocks can be arranged in one of 32 different ways called algorithms (more on them later). Signal flow is *vertical* in a DX7 block diagram. The output of an operator is shown as a vertical arrow leaving the bottom of an operator block. Each operator in the bottom row of a diagram is called a **carrier.** Any operator that is a carrier is an audio source: its output will be heard. Operators above this bottom row are *controllers.* They are referred to as modulators in FM terminology. Each of these **modulators** controls the frequency of another operator (that, of course, is what FM is all about!).

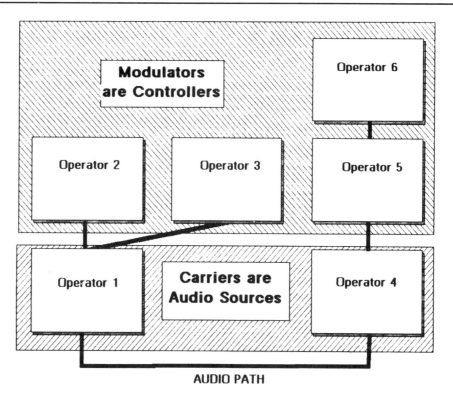

FM BLOCK DIAGRAMMING

**FREQUENCY
MODULATION**

Operator Tuning

There are two tuning modes on the DX7: **fixed frequency** and **ratio.** In either mode there are both fine and coarse adjustment selects a basic that this instrument differs from other synthesizers is that its tuning is numerical.

In the fixed frequency mode, the course adjustment selects a basic frequency range (1, 10, 100, or 1000 Hertz). The fine adjustment allows frequencies in between these ranges to be selected.

The keyboard is automatically disconnected from the operator's frequency control in this mode, hence the name, FIXED frequency. This is demonstrated in the tape.

As we will see, the ratio tuning mode is the most useful mode for FM applications. In this mode, an operator is tuned in intervals that correspond to the *harmonic series.* The number 1 corresponds to standard "A" 440 Hz. Any harmonic interval from 1 (fundamental) to 31 can be selected. It is also possible to select a tuning ratio of 0.5 as well. This is half the frequency of the fundamental, and therefore, an octave lower in pitch (See Lesson One). A fine tuning control allows the operator to be tuned to frequencies in between the harmonic series (non-harmonic tunings). In the ratio mode, the keyboard is connected to the operator.

There is also an independent **detuning** mode that allows very fine adjustments to an operator's tuning. This tuning offset is helpful for creating the chorus effect described and demonstrated in Lessons Two, Three, and Four.

FREQUENCY MODULATION

Operator Envelopes

Each operator has one envelope generator that controls its amplitude. These digital envelope generators are more sophisticated than the typical ADSR. The envelope has four variable levels, each of which can be set anywhere from minimum output level to maximum output level (0 to 99). The rate of change between each of the levels is, of course, variable. A setting of 99 is the fastest rate; and a setting of 0 is very, very slow. Like all envelope generators, the order of the level changes is always the same. In this case, the change starts at level four (L4), then changes to level one (L1), then changes to level 2 (L2), then changes to level three (L3) and holds there as long as the key is down; and finally, when a key is released — it changes back to level four again.

The rates determine how quickly the output changes from level to level. Rate One (R1) is the time between the change from L4 to L1. Rate two (R2) is the time between the change from L1 to L2. Rate three (R3) is the time between the change from L2 to L3, and rate four (R4) is the time between the change from L3 back to L4.

It is possible to create many unique and useful control shapes with these flexible envelopes. In the video, several different envelope possibilities are demonstrated.

Envelope Scaling

The keyboard can be used to affect the operator envelope generators in two different ways. In either case, envelope parameters will be altered in a manner dependent upon which area of the keyboard is being played.

Keyboard Rate Scaling

Each of the four rates will become progressively slower as lower and lower keys are played. This makes it possible to simulate the types of loudness and timbre changes that occur in many instruments like pianos, vibes, and harps. (The decays of these instruments become longer for lower notes.) The total amount of change is adjustable in eight increments. It can be set for a different amount for each of the six operator envelopes.

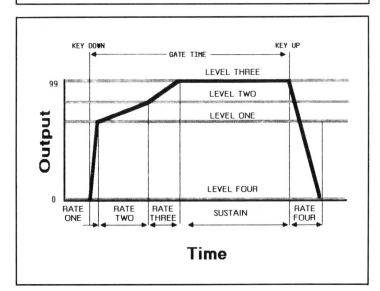

**FREQUENCY
MODULATION**

Keyboard Level Scaling

This feature raises or lowers the envelope levels for keys played on either side of a selectable key. There are three parameters associated with this function.

The **break point** is the selected key at which these changes begin. Each envelope can have its own break point.

The **curve** selects the type of progressive level change that will occur as notes are played further and further from the break point. There are four different curves possible for each side of the break point. FIG. 23.

Depth sets the maximum amount of change in level from minimum to maximum (0 to 99).

It is possible to use keyboard level scaling to get a split keyboard (among other things). This is demonstrated in the video.

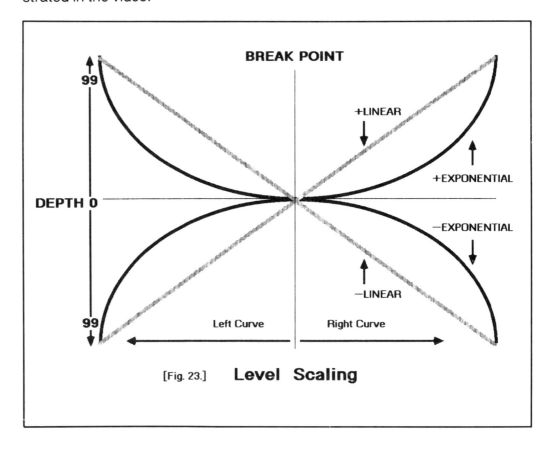

[Fig. 23.] **Level Scaling**

FREQUENCY MODULATION

Controllers

There are several controllers on the DX7. These are essentially the same as the types of controllers described in Lesson Three.

LFO

The LFO on the DX7 has six waveshapes: triangle, sawtooth, inverted sawtooth, square, sine, and random. The LFO frequency is variable. Its output can control operator frequency or amplitude. The sensitivity to pitch modulation, which is variable, is the same for each operator. The amplitude modulation sensitivity can be different for each operator.

Manual Controllers

There are several manual controllers on the DX7. The outputs of the **mod wheel, foot controller, breath controller,** and **after touch** (keyboard pressure) can each be routed to any combination of three parameters.

▶**Pitch:** The controller will determine the amount of LFO modulation of the operators' pitch (vibrato depth).

▶**Amplitude:** The controller will determine the amount of LFO modulation of the operators' amplitude (tremolo depth).

▶**Envelope bias:** The controller will determine the output level of selected operators' envelopes.

The last demonstration in the lesson shows a way to use aftertouch to control operator frequency for pitch bending with pressure. The drawbar organ demo shows the mod wheel controlling the envelope level of a "percussion stop." The displacement of the mod wheel determines the loudness of the percussion in the organ sound.

The DX7 keyboard is also *velocity sensitive.* The speed at which keys are depressed can alter an operator's output level. There are eight selectable sensitivity settings of this parameter for each operator.

Pitch Envelope

The **pitch envelope** has the same parameters (four rates and four levels) as the operator envelopes. The output of this envelope can control the frequency of all operators simultaneously. Each level can be set anywhere between 0 and 99. Level settings at 50 produce no pitch change. Level settings above and below 50 will cause the operators' pitch to go sharp and flat respectively. Keyboard rate and level scaling are not available for this envelope.

Bender

The bender on the DX7 is a spring loaded wheel. It has a variable range that is adjustable in semitones (from a half step, through an octave). The bender also has a **step mode** that can be used for pitch glissandos. In the step mode, the range setting becomes the interval of the gliss. One semitone results in a chromatic octave gliss. Three semitones — a diminished scale, and so on.

All in all, there are several eloquent and flexible control possibilities on the DX7.

Additive Synthesis

Each carrier is an operator that produces a sine wave with variable frequency and amplitude. Up to six of these carriers may be used to make a composite sound. Each carrier becomes one partial in the overall spectrum. Each of these partials has its own independent loudness envelope (the operator envelope). It is very easy to tune the carriers to various harmonic or non-harmonic frequencies by using the ratio tuning mode. The video demonstrates how to combine different carriers to make a drawbar organ sound and a mallet percussion sound. This method of creating a complex waveform by combining multiple sine waves is called additive synthesis (remember the subway train and the spray paint?). FIG. 24 is a chart that shows the ratio tunings of the partials of several types of acoustic sources.

[Fig. 24.] **Partial Structures**

Partial	Brass	Vibes	Electric Piano (Reed)	Electric Piano (Tine)	Tympani	Clarinet
ONE	1	1	1	1	1	1
TWO	2	2.70	6.25	13	1.42	3
THREE	3	6.75	17.40	—	1.53	5
FOUR	4	—	—	—	1.77	7
FIVE	5	—	—	—	1.94	9
SIX	6	—	—	—	—	11
SEVEN	7	—	—	—	—	13
EIGHT	8	—	—	—	—	15

**The above chart shows the significant partials
from within the first eight of an instruments spectrum**

Additive Synthesis Example

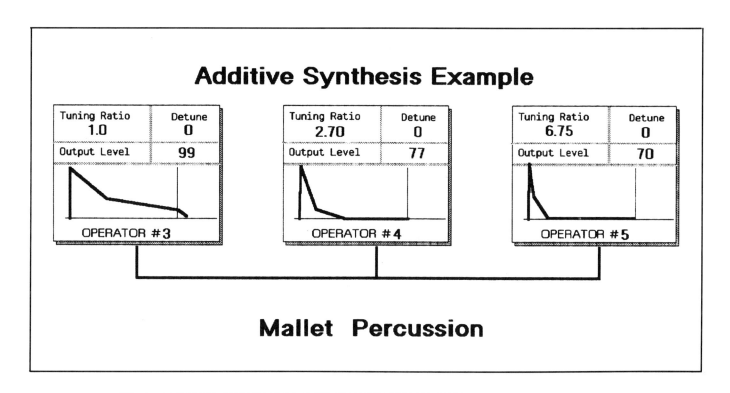

Tuning Ratio	Detune		Tuning Ratio	Detune		Tuning Ratio	Detune
1.0	**0**		**2.70**	**0**		**6.75**	**0**
Output Level	**99**		Output Level	**77**		Output Level	**70**
OPERATOR #3			OPERATOR #4			OPERATOR #5	

Mallet Percussion

Additive Synthesis Example

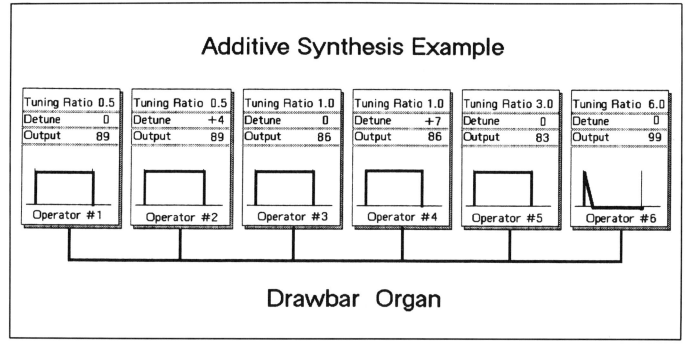

Tuning Ratio 0.5	Tuning Ratio 0.5	Tuning Ratio 1.0	Tuning Ratio 1.0	Tuning Ratio 3.0	Tuning Ratio 6.0
Detune 0	Detune +4	Detune 0	Detune +7	Detune 0	Detune 0
Output 89	Output 89	Output 86	Output 86	Output 83	Output 99
Operator #1	Operator #2	Operator #3	Operator #4	Operator #5	Operator #6

Drawbar Organ

FM Concepts

The basic "source" in FM synthesis is a pair of operators. One operator called the **modulator,** controls the frequency of another, called the carrier. The **carrier** is an audio source. As demonstrated on the tape, it is possible to use modulators as LFOs. This is sometimes overlooked as a programming possibility on the DX7. If the frequency of the modulator is below the audio range (less than 20 Hz), the result will be vibrato. In the video demonstration, notice that the rate of the vibrato (modulator frequency) remains constant throughout the keyboard range. This is because the fixed frequency tuning mode must be used for these low frequencies.

If the modulator's frequency is in the audio range, a timbre change is heard instead of vibrato. This is the foundation of FM tone production. In order to keep this timbre constant throughout the keyboard range, the interval between the carrier and modulator must remain constant for each key. This is accomplished by using the ratio tuning mode for both the carrier and the modulator.

FM is a means of producing very sophisticated timbres and timbre changes. Before we can apply our knowledge of the physics of musical sound to FM, we must find out specifically how these different partial structures are generated. Since both the carrier and the modulator have two variable parameters (frequency and amplitude), there are only four basic parameters in an FM sound.

1. Carrier Amplitude

2. Carrier Frequency

3. Modulator Amplitude

4. Modulator Frequency

The simplest way of looking at the changes caused by varying these parameters is with numbers.

Wait! Don't close the book! Contrary to what some people think, FM does not stand for "FEAR of MATH."

The mathematical relationships that effect tone production in FM sounds are very simple.

The most complicated numerical relationship used in FM sound design is a simple ratio between two numbers. A ratio is just a fraction. Musicians use ratios all the time. Time signatures, rhythmic values, and the manager's cut are all ratios.

The ratio we're concerned with in FM is the carrier's frequency relative to the modulator's frequency.

$$\frac{CARRIER}{MODULATOR}$$

This simple fraction determines the overall partial structure of an FM sound.

Side Bands

The partials in an FM sound are sometimes called **sidebands,** because they are generated above and below the carrier frequency at intervals equal to the modulating frequency. If the carrier and modulator are both tuned to frequencies that are within the harmonic series, then any resulting side bands will also be in the harmonic series as well. There are several animated spectrum plots on the video that show this.

This is the reason for ratio tuning on FM instruments. It is often desirable to tune the carrier and modulator to frequencies that are harmonically related. Ratio tuning allows the sound designer to deal

FM CONCEPTS

with simple integers (like 1, 2, 3, & 4). The two ratios 1760/880 and 2/1 are mathematically equal, but 2/1 is a much easier ratio to handle (isn't it?).

The number of sidebands generated is dependent on the depth of the modulation (in other words, the amplitude of the modulator). As the amplitude of the modulator increases, so does the number of partials contained in the FM spectrum. The amplitude is controlled by the modulator's envelope generator.

> **NOTE:** There is a variable called the **modulation index**—which is equal to the maximum amount of change of the carrier frequency divided by the modulation frequency. The modulation index is the number of audible sidebands generated on each side of the carrier. Unfortunately, because none of the available FM instruments make the modulation index available to their users, it is not easy to know exactly how many partials are in an FM tone at any given time. The number of partials determines how bright a sound's timbre is (See Lesson One). Knowing the modulation index would be helpful for setting up a basic timbre's overall brightness. Since, as in all things musical, your ears are the final judge, this is not a great inconvenience; but it would be helpful when designing sounds.

The method for figuring out which specific harmonic (or non- harmonic) frequencies will be present in an FM spectrum is very simple. The sidebands can be determined by *consecutively adding and subtracting* the ratio tuning value of the modulator to and from the carrier ratio tuning. For example, if the carrier tuning is 7 and the modulator is 1 (ratio of 7/1), then partials will be generated in the following manner.

The first sidebands will occur at the carrier (7) plus and minus the modulator (1). In other words, two new partials will be added to the spectrum at the harmonic frequencies of 8 and 6. The next pair of sidebands will occur at frequencies of 9 and 5 (plus and minus the modulator a second time). The next pair will be added at 10 and 4 (plus and minus the modulator a third time). If we continue to add and subtract the modulator tuning from the spectrum, eventually the FM timbre will have partials at the following harmonic frequencies: (8 & 6), (9 & 5), (10 & 4), (11 & 3), (12 & 2), (13 & 1), (14 & 0), (15 & -1), (16 & -2), etc. A negative sign in front of a partial indictates that it is **out-of-phase.** (There is no such thing as a negative frequency.)

The amplitude of the carrier will decrease as the modulation amount increases. Because of the combination of *in-phase* and *out-of-phase* partials, the relative amplitude of the partials constantly changes as an FM timbre develops. In effect, each partial has an individual amplitude "envelope." This produces a subtle beating effect. It can be heard in all the ratio demonstrations on the video. It is one of the unique qualities of FM timbres and is often described as a "rich" or "lively" quality. The computer animations of FM spectrums do not show these complex amplitude fluctuations. Only the average overall amplitude of the sidebands is shown.

Synth Arts

FM CONCEPTS

Carrier and Modulator Rules

The four carrier and modulator parameters are the key variable parameters in any FM sound. It is possible to make a general comparison between the changes in an FM sound caused by altering each of these variables, and the changes in the analog parameters demonstrated in Lessons Two and Three. This does not mean that FM and analog synthesizers are the same. It simply means that, in general terms, we can apply what we know about analog synthesis functions to FM functions. This is possible because both types of instruments are designed to generate and modify musical sound.

Comparison of FM and Analog Functions

Operator	Ratio Tuning	Level
CARRIER	Loudest Partial (Resonance)	Overall Loudness (Amplifier)
MODULATOR	Basic Spectrum (Waveshape)	Overall Brightness (Cut—Off Point)

102

FM CONCEPTS

RULE 1:
Carrier Ratio Tuning

In most situations, the carrier's initial ratio tuning will be the most prominent partial in an FM sound. Altering the carrier's ratio tuning will therefore alter which partial will be the loudest. This is very similar to changing the filter cut- off/resonance on an analog synthesizer. (Resonance is used to make different partials louder on an analog instrument — Lesson Two.)

RULE 2:
Carrier Output Level (Amplitude)

Altering the output level of a carrier will alter the overall amplitude and therefore, the loudness of an FM sound. This is equivalent to altering the output level of the amplifier on an analog synthesizer.

RULE 3:
Modulator Ratio Tuning

Changing the ratio tuning of a modulator will alter the overall partial structure (waveshape) of an FM sound. This will, of course, alter the sound's overall timbre. It is similar to changing the selected waveshapes of an analog source. This is one of the strengths of FM synthesis. FM can produce many more possible waveshapes than the common geometric pulse, triangle, sawtooth, and sine waveforms available on most analog synthesizers.

RULE 4:
Modulator Output Level (Amplitude)

Changing the modulator's output level (amplitude) will alter the number of sidebands present in an FM waveshape, changing its overall brightness. This is similar to altering the filter cut-off point on an analog instrument. However, the low pass filter (which is the "heart" of analog synthesis) can only alter the spectrum by removing or restoring partials "in order" above the fundamental. Another strength of FM is that changes in partial structures do not have to "pivot" around the fundamental in this manner.

FM CONCEPTS

Magic Numbers

The ratio of the carrier to the modulator is the key to FM timbre design. There are three different types of FM ratios:

1. Simple Integer Ratios

2. Complex Integer Ratios

3. Complex Non-Integer Ratios

The modulator tuning determines the basic partial structure of an FM sound.

To find out what the ratio is, in your mind (or on paper if you like), make a fraction of the carrier tuning and modulator tuning.

CARRIER TUNING to

MODULATOR TUNING

2/1

The fraction must be reduced to its *simplest form*. For example, 4/2, 1/0.5, and 7/3.5 are all equivalent ratios (2/1). This reduced form will determine the overall partial structure according to a simple set of rules.

These rules are all demonstrated in the video. Listen carefully to each demonstration. The unmodulated carrier is heard at the beginning of each note. The amplitude of the modulator is slowly increased, making it possible to hear the gradual addition of sidebands to the original carrier sinewave.

FM CONCEPTS

Simple Ratio Rules

Rule 1: If the modulator's ratio tuning is 1, 2, 3, or 4, the resulting FM timbre will always have the fundamental present. This is true even if the carrier is tuned to some other harmonic interval.

The principle behind the feed-back guitar example works as follows:

When an electric guitar feeds back, we hear a tone fade-in above the original pitch. This tone is usually an octave or a twelfth higher (2nd or 3rd harmonic partial). The wave-shape of the feed-back tone is very similar to a sine wave.

In this sound, feed-back is simulated by using a ratio of 2/1. The modulator envelope is one with in-stantaneous attack, long decay, and no sustain — momentary excitation (See Lesson Three). Because of this, when a key is depressed, we hear a timbre with a strong fundamental. As the modulation decays, we hear more and more of the carrier frequency — until eventually that's all that is left. The carrier is two times the fundamental frequency, which is (of course) one octave higher in pitch *(See Lesson One)*.

Feedback Guitar Example

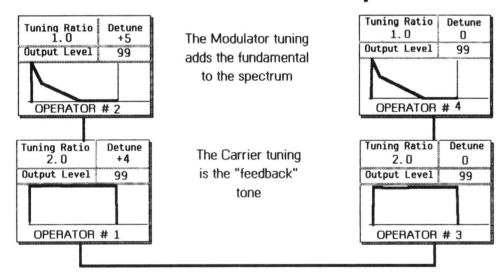

The Modulator tuning adds the fundamental to the spectrum

The Carrier tuning is the "feedback" tone

Rule # 1   Modulator = 1, 2, 3, or 4

Ratio	Order of Sideband Generation							
CARRER/MODULATOR	1st	2nd	3rd	4th	5th	6th	7th	8th
5/1	6, 4	7, 3	8, 2	9, 1	10, 0	11, −1	12, −2	13, −3
1/2	3, −1	5, −3	7, −5	9, −7	11, −9	13, −11	15, −13	17, −15
2/3	5, −1	8, −4	11, −7	14, −10	17, −13	20, −16	23, −19	26, −22
3/4	7, −1	11, −5	15, −9	19, −13	23, −17	27, −21	31, −25	35, −29

FM CONCEPTS

Rule 2: If the modulator is 1, then the resulting timbre will have all of the harmonic frequencies in its partial structure. A ratio of 1/1 will produce a timbre that is similar sounding to a sawtooth wave.

Rule # 2   Modulator = 1

Ratio	Order of Sideband Generation							
CARRER/MODULATOR	1st	2nd	3rd	4th	5th	6th	7th	8th
1/1	2, 0	3, –1	4, –2	5, –3	6, –4	7, –5	8, –6	9, –7
2/1	3, 1	4, 0	5, –1	6, –2	7, –3	8, –4	9, –5	10, –6
4/1	5, 3	6, 2	7, 1	8, 0	9, –1	10, –2	11, –3	11, –5
7/1	8, 6	9, 5	10, 4	11, 3	12, 2	13, 1	14, 0	12, –5

Rule 3: If the modulator is 2, the resulting timbre will have all of the odd harmonic frequencies in its spectrum. This produces a hollow timbre, similar to a square wave.

Rule # 3   Modulator = 2

Ratio	Order of Sideband Generation							
CARRER/MODULATOR	1st	2nd	3rd	4th	5th	6th	7th	8th
1/2	3, –1	5, –3	7, –5	9, –7	11, –9	13, –11	15, –13	17, –15
3/2	5, 1	7, –1	9, –3	11, –5	13, –7	15, –9	17, –11	19, –13
5/2	7, 3	9, 1	11, –1	13, –3	15, –5	17, –7	19, –9	21, –11
7/2	9, 5	11, 3	13, 1	15, –1	17, –3	19, –5	21, –7	23, –9

FM CONCEPTS

Rule 4: If the modulator is 3, every third harmonic partial is missing from the spectrum. This is similar in sound to a narrow (33 percent or 66 percent) pulse wave.

Rule # 4   **Modulator = 3**

Ratio	Order of Sideband Generation							
CARRER/MODULATOR	1st	2nd	3rd	4th	5th	6th	7th	8th
1/3	4, -2	7, -5	10, -8	13, -11	16, -14	19, -17	22, -20	25, -23
4/3	7, 1	10, -2	13, -5	16, -8	19, -11	22-14	25, -17	28, -20
5/3	8, 2	11, -1	14, -4	17, -7	20, -10	23, -13	26, -16	29, -19
7/3	10, 4	13, 1	16, -2	19, -5	22, -8	25, -11	28, -14	31, -17

Rule 5: Whenever the modulator is an even number, the resulting timbre will have some combination of only odd harmonic frequencies in its spectrum. This will also produce hollow sounding timbres.

Rule # 5   **Modulator = Even Number**

Ratio	Order of Sideband Generation							
CARRER/MODULATOR	1st	2nd	3rd	4th	5th	6th	7th	8th
1/6	7, -5	13, -11	19, -17	25, -23	31, 29	-	-	-
5/4	9, 1	13, -3	17, -7	21, -11	25, -15	29, -19	33, -23	-
5/6	11, -1	17, -7	23, -13	29, 19	35, 25	-	-	-
7/4	11, 3	15, -1	19, -5	23, -9	27, -13	31, -17	35, -31	-

FM CONCEPTS

Complex Ratio Rules

The term "complex" refers to the type of spectrum produced by the ratio, not the difficulty of understanding or using these rules.

Rule 6: If the modulator is 5 or more and the carrier tuning is also an integer (whole number), the timbre generated will have some combination of harmonic partials in its spectrum. The fundamental may or may not be present.

Rule # 6   Modulator = 5 or more

Ratio	Order of Sideband Generation							
CARRER/MODULATOR	1st	2nd	3rd	4th	5th	6th	7th	8th
2/5	7, -3	12, -8	17, -13	22, -18	27, 23	32, -28	-	-
3/5	8, -2	13, -7	18, -12	23, -17	28, -22	33, -27	-	-
4/5	9, -1	14, -6	19, -11	24, -16	29, -21	34, -26	-	-
3/7	10, -4	17, -11	24, -18	31, -25	38, -33	-	-	-

FM CONCEPTS

Rule 7: If the modulator is not an integer, the FM timbre will have non-harmonic partials in its spectrum. A number with digits to the right of the decimal place (like 1.45 or 3.69) is a non-integer number. Be sure to reduce the ratio to its simplest form (3.5/3.5 is really 1/1).

Modulators with .250, .50, and .750 after the decimal place are quite useful in making distortion sounds. More complex numbers like .289, or .672, or .793 produce very complex timbres that are often quite metallic sounding.

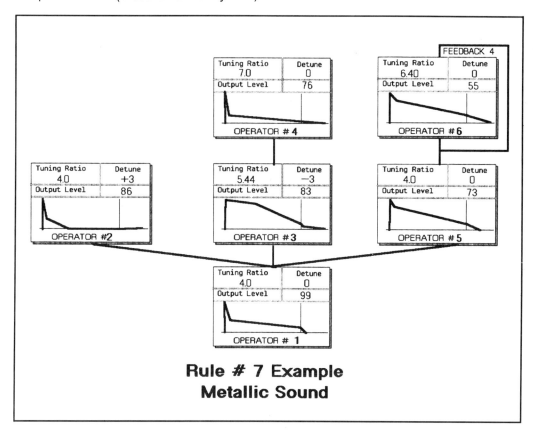

Rule # 7 Example
Metallic Sound

Rule # 7   Modulator = non−integer

Ratio	Order of Sideband Generation							
CARRER/MODULATOR	1st	2nd	3rd	4th	5th	6th	7th	8th
1/1.5	2.5,-.5	4,-2	5.5,-3.5	7,-5	8.5,-6.5	10,-8	11.5,-9.5	13,-11
1/1.01	2.01 -.99	3.02 -2.00	4.03 -3.01	5.04 -4.02	6.05 -5.03	7.06 -6.04	8.07 -7.05	9.08 -8.06
2/3.5	5.5 -1.5	9.0 -5.0	12.5 -8.5	16.0 -12.0	19.5 -15.5	24.0 -19.0	27.5 -24.5	31.0 -28.0
Special Case 1Hz/1/1	1+1HZ -1Hz	2+1Hz 1-1Hz	3+1Hz 2-1Hz	4+1Hz 3-1Hz	5+1Hz 4-1Hz	6+1Hz 5-1Hz	7+1HZ 6-1Hz	8+1Hz 7-1Hz

FM CONCEPTS

Special Cases

Here are some little known, but useful applications of ratio tuning.

Slightly detuning a modulator will create a timbre with out of tune harmonic partials. This can be useful when trying to stimulate piano-like timbres, because the enormous tension on piano strings causes their upper harmonic partials to be out of tune. (A modulator can be detuned with the fine tuning control or the detune function.) Just a slight amount of detuning will cause an audible shift in the spectrum. The partial produced by the carrier frequency will remain constant. If the carrier's ratio tuning is 1, the fundamental will be in tune and all of the other partials will quite noticeably be out of tune. This can be used for a "honky tonk" effect.

A **stacked modulator** (FIG. 25) tuned to a low frequency in the fixed frequency mode, can be used to very subtly shift all of the partial frequencies except the carrier frequency. This produces chorus-like effects very difficult to obtain any other way.

Another useful technique takes advantage of the beat phenomenon described in Lesson Two. When a carrier is tuned to a low frequency in the fixed mode, and is controlled by a ratio tuned modulator, the resulting sound will have a very pronounced tremolo at exactly twice the frequency of the carrier. In other words if the carrier is tuned to 1 Hz., the resulting sounds' amplitude will smoothly fluctuate at a rate of 2 times a second. This beating effect will have a consistent rate throughout the keyboard range. If a stacked modulator is used, the timbre of the sound can be determined as though it were a simple FM source (FIG. 25). It is possible to achieve the effect of having 32 independent LFO sine waves controlling amplitude in this manner!

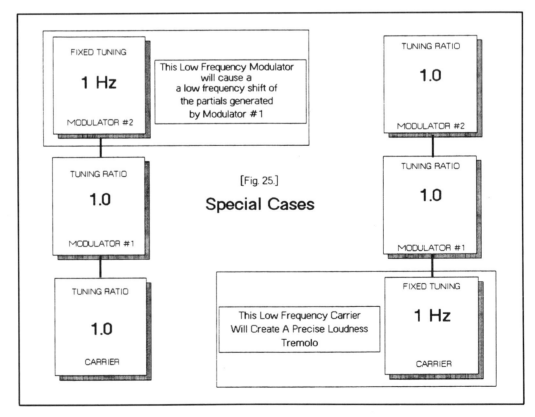

FIXED TUNING

1 Hz

MODULATOR #2

This Low Frequency Modulator will cause a a low frequency shift of the partials generated by Modulator #1

TUNING RATIO

1.0

MODULATOR #2

TUNING RATIO

1.0

MODULATOR #1

[Fig. 25.]

Special Cases

TUNING RATIO

1.0

MODULATOR #1

TUNING RATIO

1.0

CARRIER

This Low Frequency Carrier Will Create A Precise Loudness Tremolo

FIXED TUNING

1 Hz

CARRIER

Algorithms

An **algorithm** is an exact procedure that will produce a very specific and predictable result. The recipe for making a devil's-food cake is an algorithm. Computer programs, the rules of counterpoint, and all of the block diagrams in this manual, are other examples of algorithms. As mentioned earlier in this lesson, the six operators of each DX7 voice can be combined in 32 different ways. Yamaha calls each of these combinations an algorithm. The operators in each algorithm are grouped together to form sources of FM sounds. A particular algorithm may have between one and six sources.

In our FM examples so far, we have been using a single pair of operators (one carrier, one modulator). This is a simple FM source. Since there are six operators on the DX7, it is possible to have up to three of these simple sources per voice on the instrument. A complex FM source has more than one modulator per carrier. It is possible to have a complex FM source with one carrier and five modulators.

In general, there are two different types of algorithms used on the instrument. **Simple algorithms** use simple FM sources. **Complex algorithms** use complex FM sources.

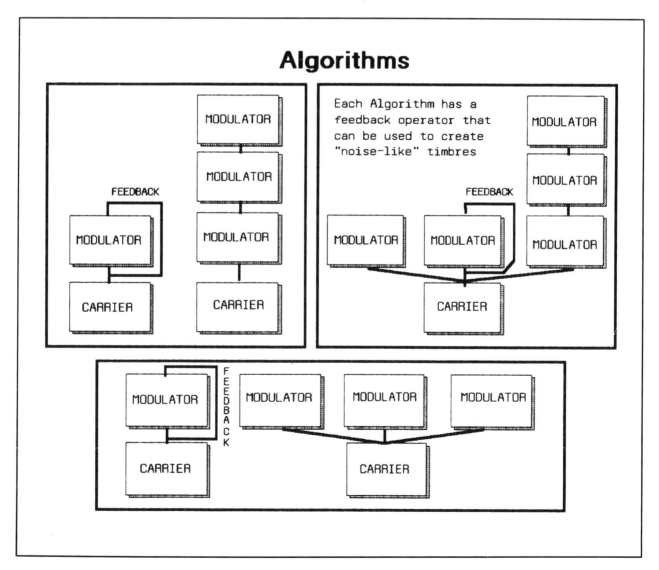

Algorithms

Each Algorithm has a feedback operator that can be used to create "noise-like" timbres

ALGORITHMS

Simple Algorithms

The first example of a simple algorithm sound on the tape uses three simple FM sources (FIG. 26). As you can hear in the demonstration, the first source has a different timbre (ratio 3/1) than the other two (1/1). Sources 2 and 3 are identical in timbre, but they are detuned to produce a chorus effect (Lesson Three). When these three independent sources of FM sound are combined, a composite waveform is produced.

The second example again uses three independent simple FM sources (FIG. 27). The organ sound is made with two simple sources. The first source, with a ratio of 1/2, produces a hollow organ timbre (odd harmonics). The second source uses a single carrier with a ratio tuning of 3 and a percussive envelope to simulate a percussion stop.

The third source uses a ratio of 1/1 (actually the ratio is — 0.5/0.5 — which is of course equal to 1/1) to produce a bass-like sound an octave beneath the organ fundamental. As you can see from the demonstration, the keyboard level scaling feature is used here to create a "split" keyboard — bass in the left hand, organ in the right hand.

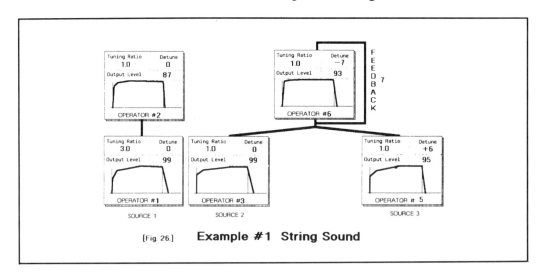

[Fig. 26.] **Example #1 String Sound**

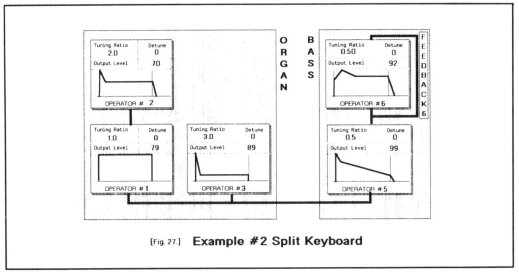

[Fig. 27.] **Example #2 Split Keyboard**

ALGORITHMS

Complex Algorithms

There are two kinds of modulator connections possible in a complex FM source. When more than one modulator each controls the same carrier, they are said to be **parallel modulators.** In this configuration, the spectrum of the FM sound will be the addition of the spectrums produced by each modulator ratio. If each modulator is a whole number, there will be only harmonic frequency partials in a sound. The envelope of each modulator can have different rates and levels. This makes it possible to create very interesting timbre changes in a sound by "layering" different spectrums on top of each other.

The other type of complex FM source uses modulators in **"stacks."**

Stacked modulators will always produce complex non-harmonic partials regardless of their ratio tuning. This occurs because sidebands are generated for each partial within a spectrum.

The sitar sound used to demonstrate stacked and parallel modulators on the video uses parallel modulators to emphasize different harmonic partials in the timbre. The velocity sensitivity for each parallel modulator is different. This is one way of creating dynamic timbre changes with the DX7. The stacked modulator is also velocity controlled. When a note is struck very quickly, its output level is very high. The strong non-harmonic partials that this produces simulates the "twang" of the metal strings of a sitar.

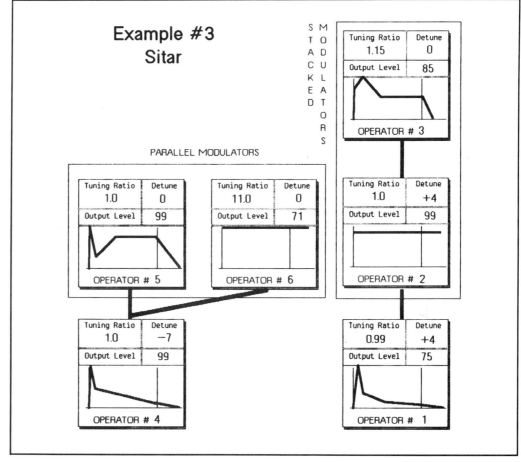

NOTES:

Synth Arts

GLOSSARY

ADSR — typical envelope generator, its variable parameters are: A = attack rate; D = decay rate; S = sustain level; R = release rate

after-touch — see pressure

algorithm — an exact procedure that will produce a specific, predictable result; one of 32 fixed combinations of six operators on the DX7

amplifier — device used to control the amplitude of an audio signal

amplitude — the vertical distance between two peaks in a waveform

analog — a circuit that produces a continuously changing electrical signal

arpeggiator — will "automatically" arpeggiate the notes of a chord

articulation — the ability to control the duration of a sound's overall pitch, timbre, and loudness; the basic skill of stating a melody

attack rate — the rate of change between the first two levels of an envelope generator

audio — electronic signals that are meant to be converted into sound waves that range between 20 Hertz and 20,000 Hertz

audio modulation — controlling the amplitude or frequency of a source oscillator with the amplitude of an oscillator whose frequency is in the audio range

audio path — the flow of audio signals within a synthesizer

band-pass filter — removes frequencies above and below the cut-off point

basic timbre — the overall partial structure, and therefore tone color, of a sound

beating — the loudness fluctuation caused by phase cancellation and reinforcement when two or more audio sources are mixed together

bender — manual controller used to bend pitch, sometimes used to raise or lower filter cut-off as well

block diagramming — use of graphic blocks to show inter-connections within a synthesizer

break point — selected key at which envelope levels are raised and/or lowered on the DX7

breath controller — manual controller whose output varies depending on how much air is forced into mouthpiece

carrier — the source of an FM sound; on the DX7 the carrier is an operator

chorusing — amplitude and timbre changes caused by combining two or more, closely tuned, audio sources together

115

GLOSSARY

clock — an LFO used to control the rate of operation of other devices such as, arpeggiators and S/H

complex algorithms — FM configurations on the DX7 that use more than one modulator per carrier

continuous excitation — tone production caused by the constant application of force such as breath or bowing

contour generator — see envelope generator

controllable parameter — a parameter whose value can be altered by a controller

controllers — a synthesizer function whose output is used to alter the value of a parameter of another synthesizer function

control processor — a modifier that alters a control signal

control signal — the output signal of a controller

curve — selects the type of progressive level change that will occur as notes are played further and further from the break point on the DX7

cut-off frequency — the frequency where selective attenuation begins in a filter

cut-off point — see cut-off frequency

cycle — one complete vibration of a sound source

decay rate — rate of change from peak level to sustain level in an ADSR

decibel (dB) — a scale used to measure relative loudness levels that compensates for the non-linearity of perception

delay — a variable control that "fades in" the amount of modulation depth with the attack of a note

depth — a general term for the amount of modulation

detuning — the altering of the pitch of one source against the pitch of another by very small amounts

digital — circuit that uses a stream of numbers to represent changing values; these numbers are converted (with the assistance of a micro processor) into an electrical signal

digital envelope generators — similar to analog only rates and levels are generated with digital numbers; a typical digital envelope has several variable rates and levels

displacement — the distance from a vibrating object and its original "at rest" position

GLOSSARY

dynamics — the ability to articulate with smooth or abrupt changes in any, or all of the Big Three; dynamics such as crescendos or pitch bends give life to the phrasing of melody

emphasis — see resonance

ensemble effect — see chorusing

envelope bias — control of operator envelope levels on the DX7

envelope generator — a synthesizer controller used primarily to simulate various types of articulation of loudness and timbre

expander — synthesizer that can be remotely controlled from another instrument's master controller

filter — a synthesizer modifier used to modify waveshape by selectively removing partials from a wave's spectrum

fixed frequency tuning — a tuning mode on the DX7 that disconnects the keyboard from the operator

FM synthesis — a method of synthesis that creates and controls timbre by modulating a source waveform's frequency with the amplitude of an audio modulator

foot-controller — manual controller to be used to directly control variable parameters

foot-switch — manual controller to be used to select (or turn on and off) features

frequency — number of cycles of a wave that occur during a fixed amount of time

gate — a control signal that corresponds to the length of time a key is held down

generators — functions that are the original source of audio or control signals, i.e., oscillator; ADSR

harmonic series — a natural series of pitch intervals whose frequencies are 2, 3, 4, etc., times the fundamental's frequency

Hertz — unit of measurement of frequency corresponding to cycles/second

high-pass filter — attenuates frequencies below the cut-off point

Hz — abbreviation of Hertz

intensity — measurement of the power of a sound wave's amplitude

inverted envelope — an envelope whose output is exactly opposite the normal envelope

GLOSSARY

key code or keyboard CV — a control signal that identifies which particular key, and therefore, pitch, is held down

kHz — abbreviation of kiloHertz

kiloHertz — unit of measurement of thousands of cycles/second

layering — see stacking

left hand mute — lowers the loudness of the sound on the left side of the keyboard of the JX 3P

LFO rate — the operating frequency of an LFO

loudness — the subjective parameter of sound related to a wave's amplitude

Low Frequency Oscillator — a synthesizer generator whose output can be one of several selectable waveforms; the range of frequencies of its output is generally below 20Hz

low-pass filters — attenuates frequencies above the cut-off point

manual controllers — mechanical devices that give a performer direct physical access to synthesizers, i.e., keyboard, guitar, etc.

master controller — main area of physical interaction between the performer and the synthesizers, i.e., keyboard, guitar, etc.

MIDI — Musical Instrument Digital Interface

mod controller — manual controller used to control amount of LFO

mode — used to denote various types of filters

modifiers — synthesizer functions that alter signals generated by sources or controllers

modulation — the ability to periodically vary pitch, timbre, or loudness over the course of a single duration, i.e., vibrato and tremolo: in synthesis — changing a parameter with a controller (typically an LFO)

modulation index — an FM variable equal to maximum amount of change of the carrier frequency divided by the modulation frequency

modulator — a general term for a controller; in FM a modulator is an audio modulator used to control the carrier frequency — producing sidebands

mod-wheel — see mod controller

momentary excitation — tone production caused by plucking or striking

noise generator — a synthesizer source of unpitched sound

notch filter — removes a narrow band of frequency at the filter's cut-off point

GLOSSARY

octave — basic pitch interval that can be represented with a frequency ratio of 2/1

operator — the basic FM function on the DX7; the digital equivalent to a sine wave generator, an amplifier, and an envelope generator

oscillator — a synthesizer source which produces geometric waveforms at various frequencies

pan-pot — can place a sound anywhere within the stereo field

parallel modulators — an FM configuration where more than one modulator directly control the same carrier

partial — the individual sine wave components that make up a complex waveform's spectrum, and therefore, timbre

pattern — see waveform

peaks — the highest and lowest points of a wave

period — see cycle

periodic vibration — cycle of perfectly repeating motion caused by the interaction between restoring force, displacement, and momentum

phase — the relative displacement in time between the starting points of two or more waveforms of the same frequency

Phase Distortion — changes a wave's partial structure by literally altering the shape of the wave itself

phase filter — a type of filter that shifts the phase of frequencies on one side of the cut-off point

pitch — the subjective parameter of sound related to a wave's frequency

pitch envelope — envelope that controls the pitch change of a source

poles — particular component configuration within filters that determines the steepness of a filter's roll-off

pressure — (after touch) control signal with an amplitude directly related to the force applied to the key while it is held down

processors — alter signals, but generate no signals by themselves; see modifiers

programmable — synthesizer values that can be stored and recalled digitally

propagation — the transfer of energy through a medium

pulse width — the measurement of the duty cycle of a rectangular wave

Q — see resonance

119

GLOSSARY

quantize — to change a smooth shape into a series of discrete steps

rate — generally refers to the frequency of an LFO

ratio tuning — the ratio of the carrier frequency to the modulator frequency in an FM sound

release rate — rate of change from sustain point back to starting point when a key is let up

resonance — a parameter of filters that increases the amplitude of frequencies near the cut-off point

restoring force — the force that tends to return a vibrating object to its equilibrium position; restoring force increases proportionately with displacement

ring modulator — a specialized amplitude modulator that produces an output that contains only the sum and difference frequencies of its input waveforms' partials — generally used to create metallic, non-harmonic, timbres

roll-off — the attenuation curve from the cut-off point of a filter; the steepness of the curve is dependent on the number of "poles" in the filter circut

sample and hold — a synthesizer controller that creates quantized variations of its input waveform

sawtooth wave — a geometric wave with partials at all of the harmonic frequencies; it has a bright, brassy sounding timbre

selectable features — features of a synthesizer function that are typically associated with on/off or multiple choice switches, such as range, waveshape, sync, etc.

sequencer — function that can remember and repeat a keyboard performance

sidebands — the partials generated by Audio Modulation

simple algorithms — FM configurations with only one modulator per carrier

sine wave — the simplest periodic waveshape — its spectrum contains only the fundamental frequency; sine waves have a very pure, dull timbre

slope — see roll-off

slow attack — a gradual level change that occurs at the beginning of a sound

sound wave — a disturbance that is capable of eliciting the sensation of hearing in humans; caused by objects vibrating with frequencies and amplitudes within the limits of human perception

sources — general term for synthesizer functions that generate audio signals; every instrument has at least one source of sound (some type of vibrating body that is set in motion by the player; it may be a taut string, a bamboo reed, a stretched string, a column of air, or some other vibrating object that is responsible for the basic waveshape produced by an instrument)

GLOSSARY

spectrum plot — a graph showing the relative frequency/amplitude of the individual partials in a complex waveform

split keyboard — ability to assign different sounds to upper and lower sections of a single keyboard

square wave — rectangular waveform with a spectrum containing only odd harmonics; square waves have a hollow sounding timbre

stacked modulator — a modulator that is used to control **another modulator** in a complex algorithm

stacking — play all voices in an instrument from a single key hit

step mode — quantized pitch bending on the DX7

stereo chorus — detunes and delays one side of the final audio signal

style emulation — the ability to imitate the performance style of a player as well as the sound of an instrument

sub-oscillator — alternative oscillator output with a frequency of one half of the oscillator's true tuning (one octave lower in pitch)

subtractive synthesis — the creation of sounds by removing partials from the spectrums of complex waveforms

sustain rate — the envelope level that will "hold" as long as a key is held down

tempered scale — scale that divides an octave into 12 equal pitch intervals (tempered semitones)

tempered semitones — unit of measurement representing 1/12th of an octave in a tempered scale

threshold of sensation — softest sound we can hear

timbre — the parameter of sound associated with waveshape; tone color

timbre envelope — envelope used to control synthesizer's timbre

tone production — the mechanical method of generating sound on an acoustic instrument

tremolo — periodic changes in loudness or timbre

triange wave — pyramid waveshape containing only odd harmonics; a very dull timbre

variable parameters — parameters of a synthesizer function that are generally associated with a slider, knob, or range of values; filter cut-off, frequency, rate, etc.

velocity — control signal with amplitude determined by speed at which keys are depressed

GLOSSARY

vibrato — periodic changes in pitch

variable pulse — rectangular wave whose pulse width can be altered

voltage — the flow of electrons

Watt — measurement of power

wave — a traveling disturbance

waveform — a general term for a wave's pattern of motion; ie. square wave

wavelength — horizontal distance covered by one cycle of a wave

waveshape — see waveform